A Riff of Love

"Participate in an inspiring spiritual drama in search of the 'blue note,' with scales and scores which soar beyond boundaries of injustice and the underground economy. Join in this session of transformation, hopefulness, and a conversation about a strange land in a familiar neighborhood. Enderly Park is continuously fresh and engaging. Turn around once more, 'one more once' and gaze through broken windows seeing we are all one."

—Clifford A. Jones, Senior Minister, Friendship Missionary Baptist Church

"Greg . . . weaves together experiences from life in a radical Christian community with unexpected insights from his work as a saxophonist to tell a love story about the people of Enderly Park. This is one of the most human books I've read in a long while, and I heartily recommend it."

—Mark Van Steenwyk, founder, Center for Prophetic Imagination

"Greg Jarrell walks the walk through his high-poverty Charlotte neighborhood, learning the names behind the statistics, finding jazz and Jesus in their stories. If you want to hold onto prejudices about what poor people are like, this book is not for you. It's for the open-minded, and open-hearted, and for all of us who want to understand our fellow human beings a little better."

—Tommy Tomlinson, author of the forthcoming *Elephant in the Room*

"This book reads like a series of profound prayer walks, with Jarrell taking us into homes and parks and street corners we might not otherwise have access to. Through vivid, evocative language, and a propensity for connecting history to the present day, Jarrell made me fall in love with his neighborhood. There is no need quite so pressing as the challenge to learn to love our neighbors as ourselves in an unequal and unjust country such as the U.S., and Jarrell approaches this task with wisdom, humility, and humor."

—D. L. Mayfield, author of *Assimilate or Go Home: Notes from a Failed Missionary on Rediscovering Faith*

"Greg Jarrell provides readers unique insight on issues related to racism, housing segregation, gentrification, and community building from his first-hand experiences as a community organizer on the ground in Charlotte, North Carolina . . . He moves it from the theoretical to the concrete by focusing on the humanity of those impacted by racial inequality, and includes an examination of his own personal learning process."

—Bree Newsome, American filmmaker, musician, speaker, and activist from Charlotte, North Carolina

"Greg's book reads like jazz: the rhythm and flow pull you into a whole different part of your heart and mind. And that's a good thing, because it helps us be present to things we might rather avoid but need to confront for the sake of our babies, the sake of our communities, and the sake of our humanity. What a gift to take this journey."

—Sandhya Jha, author of *Transforming Communities: How People Like You are Healing Their Neighborhoods*

"Once every few years, a book appears that makes Christians and Churches notice that, Yes, we've been doing some nice and good things—but why haven't we been doing this? With simplicity, compassion, and courage, Greg shows us how to be the people of God in obvious ways we've missed. We might say this book is 'well-written,' but great writing is nothing more than great living and taking the time to tell about it. I think Jesus would say, Yeah, this is what I was talking about."

—James Howell, Senior Minister, Myers Park United Methodist Church, Charlotte, North Carolina

A Riff of Love

Notes on Community
and Belonging

Greg Jarrell

FOREWORD BY
Jonathan Wilson-Hartgrove

 CASCADE *Books* · Eugene, Oregon

A RIFF OF LOVE
Notes on Community and Belonging

Cascade Books
An Imprint of Wipf and Stock Publishers
199 W. 8th Ave., Suite 3
Eugene, OR 97401

www.wipfandstock.com

PAPERBACK ISBN: 978-1-5326-3325-6
HARDCOVER ISBN: 978-1-5326-3327-0
EBOOK ISBN: 978-1-5326-3326-3

Cataloguing-in-Publication data:

Names: Jarrell, Greg, author. | Wilson-Hartgrove, Jonathan, foreword.
Title: A riff of love : notes on community and belonging / Greg Jarrell ; foreword by Jonathan Wilson-Hartgrove.
Description: Eugene, OR : Cascade Books, 2018 | Includes bibliographical references.
Identifiers: ISBN 978-1-5326-3325-6 (paperback) | ISBN 978-1-5326-3327-0 (hardcover) | ISBN978-1-5326-3326-3 (ebook)
Subjects: LCSH: Jarrell, Greg. | Baptists—Clergy—United States—Biography. | Communities—Religious aspects—Christianity. | Church. | Fellowship—Religious aspects—Christianity. | Religion and justice.
Classification: BV4466 .J37 2018 (print) | BV4466 .J37 (ebook)

Manufactured in the U.S.A.   OCTOBER 12, 2018

For Khalil

One thought can produce millions of vibrations
and they all go back to God . . . everything does.
—JOHN COLTRANE

Table of Contents

Foreword

I WAS RAISED BY good Baptists who loved Jesus and made me memorize the Bible in the King James Version. If it was good enough for Jesus, it was good enough for us. We didn't have much in the way of money, education, or political power. But we had the Word of God, and we were going to hide it in our hearts that we might not sin against God.

When the Second Great Awakening swept across the South in the late eighteenth and nineteenth centuries, the "Bible Belt" where I come from was born. Baptist and Methodist preachers had a radically democratic message that appealed to poor people, white and black: you may not have much, they told my ancestors, but you have the Word of the Living God. Like Saint Peter outside the temple gates, addressing the beggar who asked for some change, those fathers and mothers of our faith said, "Silver and gold have I none, but such as I have, I give Thee." It's no small thing to hear from the heavens.

The Word of God is powerful—sharper than a two-edged sword, the Scriptures tell us. But the peculiar logic of the Bible is, as God says to Saint Paul, that "my power is made perfect in your weakness." But we do not like weakness. God's people are susceptible to the temptation to trust this world's power over the power of God.

In the story of American Christianity, this fundamental issue of faith cannot be separated from the story of race. The slave master who claimed to own people by divine right read the same Bible as the people who sang, "Before I'd be a slave, I'd be buried in my grave / and go home to my Lord and be free." But they did not read the Bible the same way. *How* we read the Bible has everything to do with whether we ever hear the Word of God.

This is a book about how to read the Bible. That may not be immediately clear because Greg is a musician and storyteller—a mendicant poet of the twenty-first century, wandering the streets of Enderly Park in the tradition of Francis of Assisi, Teresa of Avila, and Jesus of Nazareth. You may have thought you picked up a memoir or a series of meditations. But you deserve a fair warning: this is a book about how to read the Bible. It is written by a preacher, and a preacher is going to speak on God's behalf.

But Greg knows—and this book shows—that the Word of God is something more than the words on the page of your Bible. Of course, that text always matters. Like any good preacher, Greg pays attention to the text. But he is also immersed in a context, living in and among the people to whom Jesus comes, always proclaiming good news. The Word of God emerges from that dance between text and context, a living and breathing thing.

In the beginning, we are told, God spoke the world into existence. "Let us make the human in our image," Genesis says. Out of the community that is God's self, God speaks community into existence—"male and female God created *them*." Community thru improvisation. It was, the text says, *very* good.

But we have turned from this good news to trust other ways. Religious people are not exempt from this temptation. "Between the Christianity of this land and the Christianity of Christ, I see the widest possible difference," Frederick Douglass said in the nineteenth century. We are awash in evidence to support his claim today. Christian nationalism (the latest heir of slaveholder religion) blesses greed, celebrates cupidity, and encourages enmity toward non-white neighbors. It sets millions of people up to feel righteous about our worst sins. It pits the Bible's words against the Word of God.

How, then, can any of us hope to hear and trust the true and living Word? How can we learn to read the Bible? Greg has given us an offering to help us on our way. He has heard the life-giving Word, and he is sharing it on these pages and in his life. May you, dear reader, hear the same Word and find grace to trust it wherever you are. May you learn to improvise community with the neighbors God has given you, even as the Spirit riffs on the truth we are able to sing.

Jonathan Wilson-Hartgrove
The Feast of Paul Miki, Martyr of Japan
2017

Acknowledgments

"Man, sometimes it takes a long time to sound like yourself," Miles Davis said. Which is right. Learning what it is you have to say, and how to say it in such a way that you sound like yourself, is the work of a lifetime, the sort of thing that you do only with fear and trembling. I have been working on trying to sound like myself through written words and by playing a saxophone for as long as I can remember. I have a ways to go yet, but the work that follows is my best attempt at it for now. I hope that, if nothing else, it sounds a bit like me, and that anyone who takes the time to read it will be encouraged to keep figuring out how to sound like themselves.

Sounding like yourself is not the sort of work done by yourself, though. It takes a whole community of friends and companions to help you learn who you are and what you have to say, and to hold you accountable for saying it. I have an extraordinary gift of a wide community of folks who have helped me along the way to learn a bit more how to live into my own voice. Only the few who have had a role with this project are mentioned below, but there are many, many more whose influences echo through this work, and, I hope, in my life.

A number of people read various sections of this work and offered comments that made it significantly better, including Fred Robinson, Jeff Rose, Gale Kinney, Jonathan Jones, Brandon Wrencher, Lori Thomas, Lesley-Ann Hix Tommey, Tom Hanchett, and Ben Boswell. Anthony Smith provided much of the initial encouragement that convinced me I could write this, and has been a gracious friend and brilliant colleague along the way. And Bud Fisher is as responsible as anyone for deepening my journey of imaginative discipleship. I am deeply grateful to have him as a mentor and friend.

Several people read the entire work and made it significantly better. Bill Rogers worked with me from the very beginning, which was surely painful, but kept pushing me to make it better. I am so grateful for Bill's wise guidance and encouraging words. Coleen Muir helped me to see the first full draft into a finished product, and made it far better than I could have made it on my own. Coleen's partner Troy Conn is a brilliant musician and one of my most frequent musical collaborators. I owe their entire household a huge debt.

Thanks to Jonathan Wilson-Hartgrove for his insightful foreword, and for his witness to God's goodness in the world.

My wife Helms has been an amazing partner for nearly two decades. She has been a most helpful critic of this work and also a patient spouse and friend, all of which makes me a better thinker, writer, and follower of Jesus. This book would not exist without her as a partner, nor would it exist without her patience with me as I have completed it. I am so grateful to share my life with her, and with JT and Z.

And finally, to the QC Family Tree Youth, who keep turning me around. They inspire and enrich my life in ways that deepen our journey of discipleship. This book is dedicated to one of them in particular, but each of them matter deeply to me and matter deeply to the God we serve together.

Prologue: Track 01

Right now I am doing exactly what good white people teach good white boys like me not to do.

I am walking alone in what my peers would classify as one of the worst neighborhoods in Charlotte. It is late, nearing midnight. I do not exactly know when I will return, nor did I leave information on my whereabouts with anyone else. I am not particularly worried or especially alert. I have no way of defending myself. The first stop on my journey is to knock on the door of a house that my neighbors tell me is the local trap house. That is a residence managed by an entrepreneur in the business of pharmaceutical sales, which is to say, you can buy drugs at the trap house. They generally keep a good house party going most of the time, and I am about to crash it. My mother would not approve of this scenario.

I am not looking for a fix. I am trying to find Monique. She does not keep the most savory company. I am looking for her because I want to find her son Anthony, who is supposed to start summer camp tomorrow. He is a first-grader experiencing homelessness, and right now the likelihood is that he and his mom are temporarily staying in this trap house. The summer camp is a great offer for him, given by a local church who puts on a high-quality program for Anthony's peers every summer.

I knock on the door, a little annoyed that our planned meeting earlier did not take place. As I am knocking, the recognition that I am transgressing several boundaries is starting to work up through my body. A little sweat on the back. A tremble in the hands. Stomach clenching into knots. I am afraid. Standing still for a moment helps me to feel it. I do not want to feel this way, but fears grip tightly. They bury themselves deep in bones, arising in unexpected ways and inconvenient times. Late night at the door of the trap house is as good a place as any to contemplate these things.

There's not long to reflect. The door opens, and the guy on the other side looks back from under his flat-brimmed hat, pulled down to his eyebrows. His eyes are barely visible, but they register some fear also. I am not what he expected to see.

A gentle thickening of the Southern accent can help soften tense moments, something Southerners learn just by drinking the water here. It happens automatically, without planning or thought. "Hey man. I'm sorry to be interruptin' you this late. I'm lookin' for Monique, and I heard she might be 'round here at the moment." I have no idea how the doorman receives my stretched-out drawl. It comforts me, though.

To my surprise, he invites me in. I did not expect a welcome. I thought I may be perceived as a nuisance, or suspected as a cop ready to break up the business. "I don't know who that is," in reference to Monique, seemed to be a likely response, something to protect everyone. The best case scenario I imagined just a moment ago is that I would be left on the porch, and she would come outside. But now I am inside.

I guess every trap house proprietor has a unique style of decoration. Perhaps a sparse minimalism. Maybe shabby chic, or cool modernism. This particular one chose to go for the frat house look. The featured piece is a couch that looks to have made several laps through the secondhand store. Michael Jordan sails mid-flight above the couch. He glides over two young men staring at the flat screen across the room, choreographing its millions of pixels into a virtual football game. There is a recycle bin full of beer cans. Eco-friendly drug dealers—who knew? The lights are dim, the curtains drawn, and the noise of a rowdy card game spills in from the next room.

It all looks surprisingly fun. And it seems so normal—young adults up late playing video games and drinking cheap beer. This scene inspires fear? The house has a reputation for trouble, but there is none of that at the moment. My stomach has not unknotted itself all the way yet, but I am settling in and have decided that if someone offers me one of those beers, I'll take it.

My host walks to the back of the house, grasping the back of his jeans with his right hand as he goes to hold his pants onto his slim frame. He knocks on the back bedroom door while I lean against the front wall taking it all in. He waits, knocks again, and then finally stops being patient and just opens the door to interrupt. The folks in the room are loud, so he shouts over them, "Monique!"

Into the silence that follows, he says, "There's a white man at the door to see you."

There's that knot in my stomach again. Tighter this time. The back of my T-shirt is getting wet.

In the world I'm from, we don't say things like "white man." White is normative. It can safely be assumed. Whiteness need not be spoken. No—it ought not be spoken. Calling me a white man is not only unnecessary, it is plain old impolite. To my ears, modifiers about race are only needed when a non-white person is involved. There are Black-owned businesses, Black churches, Latino credit unions, Asian restaurants, the "ethnic" foods aisle at the grocery store, and so on, but nothing gets labelled "white." It is assumed that white is regular, normal even. The code is clear, although the specifics of it are unwritten. Whiteness should not be named. Unless, of course, one is looking to create a scene. Which is what I have here now.

Hearing "white" sends all my discomfort rushing back. I am transgressing boundaries to be in this space. All of my racial assumptions come with me, though I do not yet know about many of them. I assume a reasonable measure of safety, a safety partly assured by my whiteness. The well-known barrier that stands guard around this space is insufficient to keep me on the outside. To knock on the door is an opportunity I am entitled to, despite the fact that many of my neighbors would not dare attempt it. I bring my whole self when I knock on that door, even though there is a lot of myself I do not know about. I'm learning now.

"White." It sounds so aggressive when he says it. I wonder if this was a good idea after all, to come here and have my fragility shattered. I'm just trying to do good. But this young man, so that everybody can hear it, has named for me the obvious thing that I am hoping no one will notice. Somehow I wanted my whiteness to be the miracle salve for all racial discomfort—everybody be calm, there's a white guy here! I hold a near-religious belief that it is powerful enough both not to be noticed, and at the same time to be the reassurance of the benevolence of the universe.

I have crossed barriers to get here. My host is doing the same in return. He has stepped across one of my boundaries—one I have never been confronted with in this manner, one I scarcely knew I had. We are encountering one another in an unusual and vulnerable way. The trap house seems like a fortress from the outside. It is a place of danger. There are drugs. Word on the street is that there are guns as well. One does not just carelessly knock on the door. The house inspires fear around the neighborhood. No one knows what may be happening inside.

Now I am seeing the chinks in the armor. This place is vulnerable, and my presence is heightening the feeling of vulnerability. These people are outcasts of society. Some are homeless and are being taken in. Many have gone through the humiliation of arrest and prosecution, their bodies being taken from them and warehoused in undesirable places. They have been controlled, treated as menaces. With records and rap sheets, only illicit work and under-the-table odd jobs remain as reasonable options. Why not go into sales? There is at least the illusion of safety in this house, and if not safety then a chance to forget for a little while. I am disturbing a refuge of the heavy-laden.

I am scared and wondering whether this was the right idea. He is scared and wondering whether I will be bringing this gathering to a halt. We are acting out a drama that has been happening on this land since my ancestors first brought his ancestors here by kidnapping and rape and murder. Our bodies know this even if our minds cannot speak it. We have our parts memorized without anyone ever passing out the script. For my part, the fear of Blackness comes silently—not by nature, but by wordless teaching. No one ever told me to perceive danger in dark skin, but all my people learn the lesson and pass the test. The idea that a house party is dangerous never crossed my mind in my lily-white college. In a Black neighborhood, I suppose it to be one step from a riot.

My host has learned the script as well, though likely for him by personal experience and not surreptitious rumor. He is afraid that I may be a cop, or that I might call the cops, or that my invasion of this space is an initial step towards his eventual displacement from it by the mysterious forces of The Market. His fears are well-founded, learned through generations of experience. We are performing a drama that we did not choose, that we cannot escape. And so here we stand, afraid. We can do no other.

Trap house. Midnight. *There's a white man here to see you.*

And then Victor, a neighbor and friend whom I have known for a year or so, steps away from the card game and into the front room to see who the strange white man is. He finishes swallowing his most recent sip of beer, and shouts to the back of the house, "That's not a white man. That's Brother Greg."

1

Introduction: The Saints

THE AUDIENCE OF THOUSANDS was screaming as I moved to the front of the stage. They had all come to see The Four Tops, one of the most beloved American pop groups in history. The last song on the set list was their biggest hit, "Can't Help Myself." The men and women in the audience, young and old, had paid a steep fee to get into the Busch Gardens theme park in Williamsburg, Virginia, in part for this moment—the chance to sing along with The Four Tops. My job was to interrupt the stars for a moment.

The job description was written in my saxophone part, a job I have had off and on, a few times a year, since 2008. The horn section had been mostly concealed in the back, but following the second chorus, my part read, "Sax Solo. Eight Measures." That was it. No notes. No chords. No help. "Sax Solo. Eight Measures."

I was to run to the front of the stage where Duke Fakir, the last living member of the original Four Tops, would meet me with a microphone. While he pointed it toward my horn, I was to improvise for eight measures, give him a high five, do a little shimmy, and then dash back to my seat. There was no rehearsal of this part of the show. I got one shot.

When the time came, Duke met me there. He stopped singing, pointed the mic at my horn, and for eight measures, I improvised with the band. There were too many notes, the result of the rush of the whole experience plus my attempt to try and fit every riff I knew into a small space. But it was a thrill—I would have played eighty measures if they had let me. And then after the sax solo, Duke Fakir, member of the Rock & Roll Hall of Fame, gave me a little shout and a high five.

The discipline that trains musicians in how to fill empty measures with music in such a way that other people might want to listen is called improvisation. Improvisation is not just making stuff up, as my children might do at the family piano. Like any artistic discipline, improvisation is informed by tradition and circumscribed by a set of guidelines within which an improviser works. Students of improvisation learn skills, patterns, and strategies for playing improvised music. In the traditions of Black American music, which form the basis for almost all American music, improvisers learn particular ways of playing melodies, harmonies, and rhythms. The masters of this tradition often push outside the rules and guidelines of the tradition, but only after mastering the guidelines within it.

One of those masters was Charlie Parker, whose nickname was "Bird." Bird's creativity and technical ability made him the driving force in the development of the music of his era. Parker, a saxophonist, and trumpeter Dizzy Gillespie, were largely responsible for the movement of American music from the "swing" era of the 1930s and early '40s, into the bebop era of the late '40s and early '50s. They expanded the boundaries of American popular song beyond what anyone had ever conceived. Bird and Dizzy built on the harmonic and melodic concepts used by musicians of their time and played the material they were developing faster than anyone had played before.

One of Bird's biographers quotes him as saying, "They teach you there's a boundary line to music, but man, there's no boundary line to art."[1] Bird was legendary for his practice regimen as a young man, where he would have in fact learned to play his instrument within a set of boundaries, often for twelve hours a day. He clearly knew the usefulness of boundaries. Much of his recorded work demonstrates this. But as an artist, he also knew that he sometimes touched the transcendent, somewhere beyond the boundaries. Beauty existed there, expression beyond what just playing within the rules allowed. Sometimes those moments got captured on record, leaving a testament of his creative genius. But it was only through training his infectious energy into impeccable mastery that he could attain such heights.

This book is about life in my religious community, called QC Family Tree, and in my neighborhood in Charlotte, North Carolina, called Enderly Park. I moved to Enderly Park in 2005, shortly after my graduation from Baptist Theological Seminary at Richmond, Virginia. A small group of

1. Resiner, *Bird*, 27.

seminarian friends, including my wife Helms and me, had been conspiring and dreaming about what ministry might look like for us. We thought that living deeply into the journey of faith, for us, required us to immerse our whole lives into a place where we would be in close proximity to people that Howard Thurman called "the disinherited."[2]

We landed in Charlotte due to several job opportunities for those in our community, plus a series of family connections and deep relational roots in North Carolina. On moving day, we arrived at a house we had never seen before, and threw our lots in together. The house was on Tuckaseegee Road, in a neighborhood that, at that point, many Charlotteans did not know existed, despite its proximity to Charlotte's "Uptown" economic and cultural center. I started working with kids in an after-school program not long after I moved, and began playing saxophone in a number of bands in the evenings and on weekends. Those things helped keep the bills paid, but life in the neighborhood was, and still is, my chief vocation.

I brought with me to Enderly Park some assumptions that I did not yet know I had. I am a white, middle class, highly educated, straight man. That seems like pretty straightforward knowledge, but folks with my biographical profile tend to have little awareness of what any of those things mean. I was no different from my peers in this way. I am grateful to have had good teachers, in Enderly Park and elsewhere, to help me learn both the gifts and the wounds that I carry while inhabiting this particular body and heritage. Unpacking some of the assumptions I brought, and looking at how they kept me, and still keep me, from communion with my neighbors is part of the work I am doing in this book. That work is part of a lifelong journey of learning to turn around—that is, to be converted into the way of Jesus—so that I can better be of service to the work of God in the world. I hope that my work is a gift to the church, particularly during a time when Christian witness is being negated in the United States by its alliance with empire.

I came to Enderly Park with the basic disposition that I had much to learn. Though in 2005 I could not name what I needed to learn with much specificity, I possessed the nagging sense that the conceptions of discipleship I arrived with were insufficient. I knew that the discipleship offered to me in my Southern Baptist upbringing had a number of blind spots. This was especially true in how I was trained to think about racial, economic, and social issues. I caught a glimpse of the shortcomings of the discipleship of my childhood during two summers as a college student in East St. Louis,

2. Thurman, *Jesus and the Disinherited.*

IL, usually considered the poorest city in the country. I had learned that sharing the "good news" in order to "save souls" was the chief aim of my mission from Jesus. But I saw in East St. Louis that any news that claimed to save an individual with a "personal Lord and Savior" but could not alter the destiny of a bombed-out, desolate city in the richest country in the world could not be all that good.

Not long after my experiences as a college student in East St. Louis, I began seminary at Baptist Theological Seminary at Richmond, VA. The theology of white progressives that comprised much of my seminary education offered an interesting alternative, but it still lacked a compelling vision of discipleship for body, mind, and soul. My first day of seminary was September 11, 2001. While planes were being used for terror, I was in Hebrew class. Being in classes to learn how to think about the Bible and about Christian mission seemed like the right place to seek a faithful understanding of the world during such a scary time. But the resources white progressives offered did not translate into radical discipleship. Those resources proved impotent as the church in the United States failed to mount any cohesive or effective challenge to immoral and unjust wars in Afghanistan and Iraq. Whatever gifts white mainline and progressive theologies possessed for Christians, the moral formation needed to resist the call of empire was not one of them.

In Black churches I had visited, though, and in the Black neighborhoods where I had lived and worked and been welcomed with gracious hospitality, I could see that different sorts of moral formation were happening. They were as diverse and complex as the white theologies I had learned, but with different roots and different fruits. During my time in East St. Louis, and in the housing projects of Richmond where I worked as a seminarian, I witnessed hospitality and vitality unlike anything I had experienced before. Like the disciples at Emmaus, I was frightened and bewildered, but I knew I was encountering something holy. It was made known to me as I broke bread with neighbors. I needed to understand what I saw and experienced in those places, and to let that understanding work into my whole self. Discipleship could not be only an intellectual exercise, nor could it be about tallying conversions.

The blessed saints who raised me in faith during my childhood had taught me to love the Bible, and they instilled deeply in me the two greatest commandments, "to love the Lord my God with all my heart, and all my mind, and all my soul, and and my strength, and . . . to love my neighbor as myself."[3] I figured that the next step for me to deepen my faith was to find some new teachers. My new instructors would be the downtrodden, the disinherited, and the oppressed, and to maximize my learning opportunities, I would move in next door to them. I suspected I could do some good also, but this was a self-interested move. I knew I had something to gain, something I needed.

I knew when I moved to Enderly Park what the basic demographic profile of the neighborhood was. Almost all of my neighbors were Black. Almost all of them were poor. (This was true when I moved in 2005, and is true as I write in 2017, though signs of change are afoot now, which will be a subject later in the work.) In the sorts of categories that demographers measure, Enderly Park does poorly. The median income here is about 35 percent of the median income in Charlotte as a whole. Our children perform worse in school and graduate at a lower rate than their peers around the city. Unemployment is very high. Health outcomes are poor. The average age of death is ten years less than the city average, and twenty-one years less than the wealthiest neighborhoods in the city. The rate of violent crime is well above the rest of the city. In these demographic terms, Enderly Park was one of multiple neighborhoods just to the west of downtown Charlotte that were nearly identical. An entire swath of the city was suffering with these sort of outcomes, and those outcomes had remained consistent for decades. In other words, children here were born poor, and they lived poor, and they died poor, and they did everything within sight of magnificent skyscrapers they could never access.

Neighbors in Enderly Park and across west Charlotte knew that getting ahead here was nearly impossible. The economic plight of their children, in most cases, was scripted from their birth. They said as much, and in various ways, but those with political, economic, and religious power would not slow down to listen and understand. Folks in different neighborhoods, whose children had very different economic scripts ahead of them, could not believe it. The daily views of those gleaming bank towers, the professional sports teams, the growing roster of fine restaurants, entertainment opportunities, shopping destinations, and cultural establishments, and the overwhelming number of nonprofits dedicated to every possible cause convinced people across town that the problem was not so bad. Whatever poor folks wanted, it was clearly here for the taking.

---

3. Matt 22:37–40.

But in 2014, news broke that finally disrupted that narrative. A group of researchers from Harvard University and Stanford University had taken on a long-term study looking at economic opportunity in the metropolitan areas of the United States. They examined data over several decades, seeking to understand social mobility. By social mobility, they meant the ability of persons within one economic class, measured in quintiles (groups of 20 percent), to move into a different class. They especially wanted to know about the ability of people in the lowest quintile to move upwards.

The study (called the Chetty study for lead researcher, Raj Chetty) found that, in terms of the ability of its poorest residents to move from the lowest quintile of class to the highest, Charlotte finished last among the large metropolitan areas of the country.[4] Fiftieth out of fifty. Only one of every twenty-three, or 4.4 percent of children born into poverty here, moved at some point into the highest quintile of earners. Charlotte ranked behind Rust Belt cities like Detroit, St. Louis, and Cleveland, typically the places one might assume would have the lowest social mobility. Cities across the South scored poorly, and lustrous, promising Charlotte, New South city on the rise, came dragging up the rear.

The shine was off the bank towers. The wealthy here could not believe it and found it embarrassing. After decades of cultivating a gleaming image, Charlotte was unmasked. But the Chetty study served as confirmation for poor people. They already knew what the study confirmed. Getting ahead in Charlotte, North Carolina, was—and still is—more difficult than in any other place in the country.

Enderly Park is an opportunity desert. I did not know it when I moved here, but our little community relocated into the most opportunity-poor environment in the country. The kids we love are born poor, and they live poor, and they die poor. There are many factors that reside outside our neighborhood that make it so. Any understanding of the neighborhood has to keep this basic reality at the center. But the difficulty of getting ahead is not the fullness of life here. There are many other narratives that make Enderly Park the kind of soil where I want to be planted.

Life in Enderly Park is tightly circumscribed by a set of societal norms and political and economic realities that restrict the ability of neighbors to achieve economic self-sufficiency. This is where the practice of improvisation begins—with a set of tight restrictions that, in art, eventually lead to

---

4. A wealth of information about this project is available at http://www.equality-of-opportunity.org/.

a way to break boundaries. Another task of this book is to weave into its stories a picture of the neighborhood that shows the everyday brilliance of my neighbors, whose resilience in the face of oppressive circumstances creates beauty in a dry land. As improvisers, often with few tangible resources to draw from, they use a limited palette to create beautiful community.

I think the stories that follow are enhanced by drawing on music and the language of music. Part of this is personal. I am a musician who has spent much of my life practicing the craft of improvisation. I think in the way of an improviser, by weaving together loose, and sometimes unrelated, strands into a narrative. I hope that the story I am telling unites those strands in a way that echoes the complexities of life in Enderly Park, and that shows how being a part of life in this place offers both uncommon joys and deep sorrows.

In addition to the personal, I want this work to be deeply connected to the cultural heritage of the people with whom I spend my days. Part of that cultural heritage is the jazz tradition, a tradition I have studied and worked in professionally since I was a teen. Jazz came from the blues. Both were born in the heat of oppression. The heritage of Black American music is not my own, but it is part of the heritage of my neighbors. It holds not only brilliant improvisation, but also the stories of a people who "have come over a way that with tears has been watered." I hope that my engagement with that music will deepen the stories and reflections within.

There are a few characters who are important to this work and who need a quick introduction for what follows. They are saints who have come marching into my life and are responsible to a great extent for any goodness that I am part of. Their lives animate these pages, and my imagination.

Jennifer Helms Jarrell, whom most everyone calls Helms, is my wife. We were married in 2001, after meeting in college. She loves people fiercely, and brings an artist's eye to every situation. Everything is a canvas to her.

My favorite project that Helms has worked on hangs on the mantle above our fireplace. It is a series of mixed media icons that depict our neighbors as saints. On the top is Samia, an angel of annunciation. To the left is Granny, posed as Moses, ready to lead the neighborhood out of Pharaoh's house. On the right are Ricky, with a basin and towel for foot-washing, and Brother Frank as Simon of Cyrene, carrying the cross. Helms has made our home into an altarpiece that is lovely beyond words.

Helms and I spend much of our time in Enderly Park with youth and children. The soundtrack of our days is a series of knocks on the door. Often, on the other side is a young person. We organize much of our lives around engaging with those young people in ways that build their ability to develop their households and their neighborhood for themselves. Those efforts include a summer literacy camp through the Children's Defense Fund's Freedom School program, a pottery studio that makes and sells ceramics, and lots of time engaged in the sort of things young people do. We bike, and hike, and play football, and eat pizza, and go to museums, and while we do all that, we listen to and take care of each other. A number of the young people of Enderly Park appear in the following pages.

One friend whose journey encapsulates the life of the neighborhood is Curtis. He is Enderly Park's Minister of Sanitation. Each Wednesday, Curtis spends an hour or two rolling garbage cans out to the street for pickup on Thursday morning. He stops by all of the QC Family Tree houses, along with a dozen others, most of them the homes of elderly people who need some assistance. When I was preaching in a church regularly, he listened to my sermons and commented on them. When he needed some assistance, I helped him pay a few bills for his daughter in college. He stayed in our hospitality house for a while when he ran out of other options. My observations of Curtis's story weave through this work. I find him to be a captivating person, as well as someone whose story reflects the story of the neighborhood.

Victor is the loudest human on the earth. Victor could never sneak up on anyone. If you needed to launch an ambush on someone, say, to secretly plant some tomato plants in their yard, you definitely would not call Victor to help. He is also wonderfully uncouth. When we had his baptism in a backyard pool, everyone gathered around while the preacher waded into the shallow end, and said a few words about the sacred moment taking place. He then called for Victor to wade into the water. Victor proceeded to jump off the diving board and swim over to the preacher. That's Victor.

Victor is complex and interesting. He sometimes acts with deep compassion and kindness. He also makes really terrible choices at times, choices that hurt other people and himself. Like Curtis, his place in Enderly Park and west Charlotte offers a glimpse into the story of the neighborhood. He is one of the characters who, in his best moments, has helped Enderly Park to thrive, especially during lean and difficult times.

One other character is the neighborhood itself. The main thorough-fare running through Enderly Park is Tuckaseegee Road. Tuckaseegee is an extension of 4th Street in downtown Charlotte. It runs along a ridge between two tributaries of Stewart Creek. A walk through a typical block on Tuckaseegee, like the block from Rush Avenue to Pryor Street, shows some evidence of the many complex stories that are layered through the neighborhood. On the north side of the street is a vacant lot that until 2012 was a boarded-up house. The next three houses are typical of Enderly Park—medium-sized bungalows with large front porches, set back about fifteen feet from the street. They are boarded up from the inside, and have been vacant for several decades. Across the street is Mr. Torrance's stone cottage, where he has lived for almost thirty years. He raises rabbits in the back, and his two Jack Russell terriers greet everyone who walks by the front. Several brick houses stand on this side of the road, small but sturdy. Two of those have pecan trees in the front, attracting foragers each fall.

Back on the north side of the street, there are a couple of renovated houses on either side of a vacant lot. The vacant lot had a house on it until 2013. During the winter of that year, several people were using that aban-doned house for shelter. They started a fire one night to keep warm, but it got out of control and burned the house down. Now the land sits vacant, waiting for some new development. On the corner is a small brick church building, built in the 1940s. The congregation there meets on Sunday mornings, but like most congregations here has limited connections within Enderly Park during the week. The next block over features a few houses and one-story commercial buildings, some boarded up, and others housing a cultural center and health-food store, a used tire shop, a barber shop, a pub, a convenience store, and soon, a coffee shop. This block is where you can find folks tending to the business of daily life, or hanging out on a porch, or gathered at the corner store. There are almost always people around, do-ing the things that people do—talking, taking care of daily needs, looking for friends, and so on.

Those are a few of the characters along the journey. They are essential people and places in my story. Without them, I would not see or hear the world in the ways that I do. Their influence is reflected on each page of this book. However, the stories and reflections that follow are mine. I have made my best effort not to tell anyone else's story for them, but rather to observe and discuss how their friendship and influence have helped me to see myself and my neighborhood more clearly. And with the exception of Helms, I have changed the names of everyone in the book who is still living, and also obscured a few details here and there to protect folks. But they are real, and everything within these pages happened, to the best of my memory.

Two more quick statements about what follows: First, this work is organized around themes, with most chapters taking their titles from some reference to the musical world. Generally, these themes move in chronological order as well. Chapters 2 and 3 mostly concern the beginnings of my time in Enderly Park. Chapters 4, 5, and 6 form an extended lament over the loss of people and places in the life of the neighborhood. Chapters 7 and 8 are written regarding primarily regarding recent occurrences and learnings, with an eye towards the ongoing work I have to do in light of what is happening. In places where events happen outside that timeline, I have included details to help orient the reader to the timeline of the work.

Second, this is not a "how-to" work. The reader looking for a detailed manual will need to look elsewhere. I am uncertain, though, that prescriptions are very helpful in this critical time for those trying to follow Jesus in a culture that has deceived itself by claiming to be Christian while rejecting the Way of Christ. Programs will not be much good without redeemed imaginations. First we've got to get the story straight. White folks, like me, think we have been singing the Lord's song in a foreign land, but it turns out that all along we have been actors in Nebuchadnezzar's musical. I hope that the notes and songs that follow will sound like good news, especially for people, like me, who are just learning, or may not even know yet, that they are in captivity.

If I was pressed, though, to provide one practical instruction, it would simply be this: excavate your place and your soul. Within them are songs, buried, in every key, major and minor. If God's children—all of us—are going to get free from our roles and places in Babylon, and set down to walk in the abundance of life, then surely our paths will be accompanied with singing all of those songs. Here is my attempt at digging deep and listening for the music that leads to freedom. Welcome to Enderly Park.

2

Thriving from a Riff[1]

A RIFF IS A small piece of musical information. It is a few notes, perhaps four or five, not quite long enough to be a melody but at least the beginning of one. A riff is the essence of the full melody, the foundation from which a whole work is constructed.

Imagine a riff this way: The club is packed in 1930s Kansas City, home of the Count Basie Orchestra. Basie walks onto stage and strikes up the band. The bass walks, pulling out each beat on strings. The drums clang-a-lang, snare, tom, and hi-hat each doing their job. Basie sits down at the piano. He plays a riff—just a couple of notes—and looks over at the sax section. All five of them repeat it, first in unison, and then harmonizing it among themselves. The rhythm section keeps burning underneath, the drummer sizzling on the hi-hat to drive the band. The saxes keep playing the riff, holding onto the figure like a monk holds a prayer, examining each syllable. As its beauty is revealed, it starts working up into the feet of the dancers.

Basie plays another riff on the keyboard, this one in counterpoint to the first. The trombones grab it as it comes by, sliding into the groove with the second riff. The saxes call, the bones answer. Folks are getting partnered up now. The rumble of the bass is moving up past their feet, into their legs and overtaking their hips. Basie does it once more, this time for the trumpets. They glide over the top, decorating, highlighting, tying together the

1. Charlie Parker and the Be-Bop Boys. "Thriving from a Riff" is a classic Charlie Parker tune built on the chord progression of George Gershwin's "I Got Rhythm." It is also called "Anthropology."

whole. The horn sections work together as a three-in-one. They are slowly building, building, building a crescendo that seizes the soul. Each player does his part, riding the riffs with energy and precision.

Soon the whole joint is jumping. Dance floor packed, sweat pouring, Basie jumps up and points at Prez. The star sax player takes off, building from the riffs a symphony of energy and beauty. Everybody in the building, from the bandstand to the dance floor, the bartender to the doorman, gets worked into a frenzy. One shouts. Another moans when Prez hits a blue note—that's the one that tugs on the ears and rouses the conscience, the one that elicits a moan too deep for words when it hits the soul. The vibration of the bass pulsates through the floor, up through shoes and feet and shoulders and head. The drums send out an ancient call that resonates within the bones, a call so deep that it can only be answered by the hips. Prez soars above and swoops down within, growling and moaning and drawing it all upward to the sky.

When Basie's band is swinging like this, there are no words for it. You feel it with your body. You let it settle into your soul. It works on your insides, nestles in your bones, gets you from way down deep. And it all starts with a riff.

Here in Enderly Park, just two miles from the central square of Charlotte, it often seems like a riff is about all most people have. The money almost always runs out before the month does. Improvising on just the barest amount of resources is a standard life skill. One place to watch this skill come alive is in the kitchen. Freddie and Michelle are masters of this. I have walked into their house many times to see that the fridge is mostly empty. There are few cans stored on the cabinet shelves, which lack doors thanks to a lazy landlord. Their need is visible to all, but this does not stop them from offering an invitation to supper, nor does it stop the meal at their house from becoming a bounty of delight.

Freddie and Michelle like to entertain when they can. They throw big birthday parties for their kids, and every child within three blocks joins the fun. At holidays, lots of extended family come for big cookouts. Every once in a while they wind up needing to throw a rent party. These are the most entertaining. They feature a sound system and a neighbor trying to DJ. The adult beverages flow. The rules of decorum required of a child's birthday party are suspended—for Freddie, they are most always suspended—and things get a little rowdy.

Freddie's dream is to be a comic and a comedy promoter. It is more than a little late for him to get started on that career. The rent party gives him a chance to try his act out. He features himself and whoever else he can coerce or cajole into trying an amateur comedy set. These are excruciating to sit through, which also makes them endearing. The difference between being humorous in real life and being funny behind a microphone is profound. I did not recognize how different these things were until Freddie asked me to be one of his headliners. I took this as quite an honor and prepared accordingly. With just a couple days notice, I did the best I could to get some material together and practice my set. When the time arrived, my stomach was beginning to churn and my hands trembled. I've played music in front of thousands and preached for some intimidating crowds. I don't get nervous anymore, but this backyard assembly of a few dozen had my knees trembling.

I bombed. Not a single laugh. These folks wanted to laugh, wanted me to do well, and they were tipsy on top of that. If you can't make drunk people laugh, you're pretty bad.

But the rent party was a huge success, and the food was amazing. I have no idea where it came from or how there was enough. Freddie and Michelle cooked it. I know because I saw them do it and helped them carry it from the kitchen to the picnic table. The fried chicken wings were a business plan unto themselves. On the grill, Freddie elevated a hot dog to a work of art. The potato salad competed with my mother's, which is not a compliment a southern boy easily hands out. There were plenty of cold drinks to keep the party rollicking until the wee hours. A hat got passed a few times, and enough came in for the rent to get paid. Everybody got full and had a good time. But also, everybody knew why we were there, and it was not for a comedy show. The abundance on display at the party was not food and drink, but determination, and prayers, and the hard-won knowledge of how to make something out of nothing.

Just barely getting by, always living in scarcity, is not the same thing as flourishing. Thriving from a riff is possible, but if you only ever have a riff or a morsel or a crumb, the constant struggle of improvising something beautiful from nothing is exhausting. One rent party might be fun. Monthly ones are debilitating. Sitting down to supper nightly with your children and just barely having enough food to keep them satisfied can be an adventure once. Do it night after night and it chisels away at your dignity. Making a big party happen with the help of some friends by digging deep and praying for a minor miracle is a victory to be celebrated. Relying on your sons' school to feed them twice a day because you cannot afford to is a burden.

One of the miracles of life in Enderly Park is that somehow no one starves or freezes to death. Though there is no oversupply in cupboards, no children go without eating. The calories they consume are often not healthful—indeed they have long-term consequences that take years off the lives of the poor. There are many reasons for this, including both individual choices and public policy that privileges overabundant corn production over collards and peas. The decisions for that type of food supply and consumption have a cost to pay later, but in the short-term, there are enough calories for the day. The only reason this works is sharing. Rhizomes of the sharing economy here stretch far and wide. The underground economy of sharing and ensuring the wellbeing of neighbors is alive and active, happening in secret, unpublished ways.

The monetized "sharing economy" has opened up new economic possibilities around the country. Clever entrepreneurs are making fortunes off connecting people with some need to people who will share in exchange. Car-sharing services, ride sharing, bike sharing, home sharing for vacation rentals, co-working spaces—the sharing economy is inciting the imaginations of young and old alike. These are new, exciting business models for some, but in Enderly Park, the sharing economy is simply called "regular life."

"Brother Greg, I'm in a pinch right now. I'm trying to find some money to get my light bill paid."

"What did you spend your paycheck on?"

"Well, I paid my rent, but then my mom needed some help with food, and my neighbor across the street needed to get her phone turned back on. And my other neighbor is having a struggle right now with her bills, and I have to help because I hate to see her kids suffer. So now I'm a little short."

Curtis and I must have had this same conversation twenty-five times. Amazingly, his rent always gets paid, and his lights never seem to get shut off. Curtis never has enough money but somehow he makes things work. This happens because neighbors who have something share it with someone in need. They trust that when they do this, someone else will show similar kindness in their time of need.

Getting by from the kindness of neighbors sometimes fails. Curtis winds up walking through some hard times. When he fails to get the bills paid, the results can be disastrous. Bank fees rob him at a time when every dollar counts. Predatory financial services—check-cashing services, private loans, and so on—deepen the financial hole. As the hole gets deeper, temporary relief by way of drugs or alcohol becomes more and more tempting. Eventually, a life falls into chaos.

But even the disastrous is met by another example of the rich hospitality of God through neighbor. Couches and extra beds are always full in Enderly Park, as people host a neighbor in the midst of a hard time. The sharing goes deep. It has consequences. It requires sacrifice. This looks like the wisdom of an ancient way of life. Jesus says, "Give to everyone who begs from you; and do not refuse anyone who wants to borrow from you."[2] The upside-down logic of the gospel is that those whom the world despises because they have too little are near to the heart of God, who shares in their suffering and the joy of their self-emptying.

Curtis lives deeply into the good news in a way that confounds me. He does give to everyone that begs from him. I will gladly lend him some money, but I count the cost. I know that it might pinch my budget a little until he can pay me back. Curtis trusts in the same God who provides just enough for the Israelite journey across the desert into freedom. Simply walking with this God who provides in the desert, who feeds us with himself, results in proximity to the kind of neighbors who enliven the journey, even when the road is steep and dangerous. No other reward is needed outside of the chance to walk in this pilgrim way.

❧

KNOCKKNOCK. KNOCKKNOCK.

The door flies open.

This is how we mark time in our hospitality house. Two quick knocks, and then across the threshold zooms Khalil. He is an alarm clock. Khalil is here? Must be 3:15, and the bus has just dropped kids off.

Khalil is always the first to arrive in the afternoon. He pinballs across the room offering fist bumps, hugs, jokes, grins. He picks up my two boys, a sure way to win the affection of preschoolers. If I'm not paying attention, Khalil may slip them some candy, which seals their bonds forever.

2. Matthew 5:42.

For preschoolers, this is the best part of the day. A youth—old enough to admire and young enough to be a friend—showers them with affection. No matter what is happening, the sound of Khalil's voice sends JT and Z running in search of the attention they know he will provide. They are learning friendship, and Khalil is a good teacher. A tag game breaks out, maybe, or a tower of blocks gets constructed. Perhaps we all head outside to toss a football or play in the leaves. Whichever way we bounce, a sense of wonder awaits.

The streets of west Charlotte can be mean. They take our young people and harden them. They grind them down into sharp edges. They steal their imaginations and assault them with trauma after trauma. The streets rob them of the chance to carelessly explore their environment. But Khalil has resisted the meanness so far. He still has his softness, his curiosity, his tenderness. His imagination is big. He still believes he can give birth to his dreams. So many others, at frighteningly young ages, have built tall, thick walls around their psyches and their hearts. Their imaginations are alive, but kept hidden away. They have dreams, but they stop believing that they are the ones who can make them come true. This is a strategy for survival. It is a way of maintaining a sense of security when trauma can be just around the corner, in the form of stop-and-frisk policing, or a person driven to despair who feels the need to rob, or the sight of a domestic dispute taking place on the sidewalk. Anyone subject to these assaults must turn tough quickly, and children learn that soon.

Khalil has maintained a wild-eyed, childlike way of being in the world. I love that about him, and I love that he brings that out in everyone else. The boys engage in his goofy games. He gets them interested in things they would otherwise ignore. Their imaginations break free again. They get silly.

The girls adore him. With his small frame, his playful hair, his voice still high-pitched, he is their kid brother, only if they liked their kid brother. Where it might take weeks or months, even years, for me to see behind the wall with some young people—or to feel like I can fully be myself—with Khalil it is instantaneous. His play begets play. The room is more fun and interesting with him in it. He invites everyone into belonging. This is a gift for which there is no accounting. It is simply to be enjoyed.

Sharing things big and small creates connection. Khalil bubbles over with self-giving generosity. Wherever he goes, he connects with people. Curtis not only offers some hard-earned money to a neighbor, he offers a piece of himself through the work he has done, through his desire to be kind to parents who are struggling to make the bills.

In our hospitality house, we have learned that the act of sharing a meal or offering a guest room to a stranger can establish a quick intimacy. We offer the gentle care of another's body by providing protection from the cold and rain. A guest offers a gift in return by doing dishes while I help kids with homework. These are small offerings to one another that quickly build connections. Our bodies and even our homes can be, in Paul's terms, "living sacrifices," acts of worship to God. Some of our best worship experiences are simple acts of kindness in caring for each other's fragile bodies. We make our offerings to a brother or sister in remembrance of Jesus.

Life composed with mutual care and offering ourselves as gifts to one another has a rhythm to it. By sticking around long enough and paying attention, you can learn to fall into that rhythm and find a place in it. Creation teaches rhythm. There are seasons of life—times of want and times of plenty. There is time for the shedding of leaves, time for hibernation, time for new growth, time for producing fruit and harvesting. There are droughts and famines, bumper crops and floods. Households experience this as well. Good news clusters together. Bad news, my neighbors often tell me, comes in threes. The rhythms of bounty and want guide us along, by sunset and sunrise, by birth and death, by anticipating and reflecting.

In Enderly Park, one of the ways injustice shows its face is by the intervals between seasons of want and seasons of plenty. The seasons of plenty tend not to last long—there is so much need. When Curtis has a nice check with some overtime pay in it, it disappears just as quickly as his regular paycheck does. The money keeps moving. The bill collectors keep hounding. The seasons of want can last a mighty long time—the winters turn long and unrelenting. Sharing keeps people going in the short term, but it can drive them to despair in the long term. Even a robust sharing economy, with rhizomes secretly spreading across the neighborhood, cannot cover up a lack of resources. It cannot hide the plain fact that opportunity is scarce here, even as it abounds in places just a mile or two away. No one starves in Enderly Park, but plenty go to bed hungry. Families and friends double up in houses. Someone walks an hour to and from work to save on bus fare. Medicines get prioritized, some of them having to go unpurchased, whatever the consequence. There is nothing romantic about living from a riff. Neighbors say it this way: *The struggle is real.*

The struggle *is* real, and it has real and sometimes dire consequences. It takes lives from families. The Charlotte city government publishes detailed demographic data every two years about every neighborhood in the city. Those figures say that in Charlotte as a whole, the average age of death is 72 years. In Enderly Park, it is 62 years. Which means that on multiple fronts, poverty is killing my neighbors. They are dying because of the difficulty of accessing consistent health care. Exposure to toxic environmental factors is higher here. The greater difficulty of accessing fresh food, coupled with the relative cheapness of processed calories, leads to increased risk of diabetes and heart disease. Violence takes people away too soon.

"The struggle" costs my neighbors, on average, about ten years of life. That is a decade of loving your grandchildren, of singing and painting, of cooking for your family, of making love to your spouse. A decade of watching the sky explode with color during the fall. Ten opportunities to anticipate the first tomato from the garden or to light candles for visitors at Christmas.

To see in clearer detail what opportunities are lost in those missing years, or how the gift of years is made beautiful through riffs—a visit on a neighbor's porch or the sound of children jumping into piles of leaves—requires proximity. By being close enough to notice, by sticking around and paying attention, the beauty of Enderly Park begins to seize anyone with eyes to see. The crepe myrtles in flower are like pom-poms lining the street, cheering on neighbors as they head to work and school. The old house with chipping paint and sagging porch looks wise, as though it could tell stories to illumine the world.

Most neighbors here are poor, but contrary to American characterizations of poor folks as static, unchanging, pitiable characters, poor people live fascinating and complex lives. They are not problems to be solved or objects to whom to offer charity. They are the subjects of their own stories, the authors of their own liberation. My neighbors are God's people, full of beauty and goodness, comprised of interesting contradictions and peculiar brokenness. They live close to the heart of Jesus.

Those like me, who grew up with access to power and privilege by the simple fact of our whiteness, can have a hard time imagining the complex beauty of such a place, where almost everyone is poor, and almost everyone is African-American. But we know and celebrate and consume the music of the people with those complex and beautiful stories. Almost all American popular music has roots that can be traced back to Congo Square in New

Orleans, where enslaved people would gather on Sundays to remember and build the cultures threatened Monday through Saturday by their captors and their captivity. One of the musical traditions that eventually grew from that culture-building is the Blues. The Blues tradition builds meaning in a world where the hard times just won't quit.

The Blues is music, but it is not just music. It is a way of approaching life. It is a tradition that is passed down in storytelling, in music, in preaching, in the ways that bodies move and encounter one another. When regular old sense just won't do, Blues sense constructs meaning in the cruel world. The blue notes capture what Paul calls "moans too deep for words."

There is a rhythm of life, molded by the Blues, that dances across the sidewalks of Enderly Park, vibrating through the blocks and coloring both the days and the nights. Especially the nights. The streets dance with melodies composed with shades of soul and hip-hop and gospel. Life teems with joy and laughter, with rage and determination, with love and leisure. You hear it all just by stepping outside. The living is sensuous and lyrical, a teasing dance that draws you into its charms. The Blues has always been a strategy for coaxing beauty out of hard times. It is a tradition from a specific people with a particular story, but it says something universal.

In the middle-aged man walking to the corner store, you see the Blues incarnated. He is tired after a hard day's work. His body aches from a day's labor, so he moves slow. He gets there when he gets there. But though he is worn, he carries resilience in him. His back is not bowed, though his boss is too demanding, nor is his spirit cast down, though the rent man keeps meddling around. He strides with cool, walking to a rhythm only he hears but everyone sees. The Blues has taken up residence in his body. Even if you can't name it, you know it.

Echoes of drums are in his body, but not just there—they are everywhere. Teen boys beat on furniture. A car stereo rattles the whole frame of its vehicle. A church choir rehearses with the doors open, and heaven fills the streets. Heaven sounds like a clap and a stomp and a tambourine, always the sound of skin stretched over a frame, any available frame, the skin taut though worn. Flesh on flesh, shoe pounding floor, air rushing through throat—the sounds call out the ancient, bone-deep secret that this is what home sounds like. Here is an age-old reminder of who we all are. Even those like me, whose bodies have long forgotten the distant call of the drum, begin to feel the vibrations pulsing, bumping, aligning with heart, feet, hips, echoing around to long-forgotten places within. The struggle is real. The blues is real-er.

So have there always been riffs of drum and melody to nourish the resistance, to straighten the spine for what is to come. In the hush-harbor, enslaved people sang a simple song with deep theology: "O Mary, don't you weep, don't you mourn—Pharaoh's army got drowned-ed." In face of trials and want, a little riff will do. A song ushers in a new world. KnockKnock. ThumpThump. Rat-a-tat-rat-a-tat. The rhythms of the heavens rupture the world.

Songs build worlds. They educate, inspire, and create cultural identification. Music binds tribes together. It tells a people's story. But people cannot eat songs. Songs may nourish movements, but bodies need fruits and vegetables. In Enderly Park, the need for basics—food, warm clothing, decent shoes, quality shelter—is on display right alongside the resilience and creativity that keeps people singing their lives. In a place where it often seems there are too few meals, still there is enough. There could be more, and probably should be more, but because a spirit of abundance lives here, there is enough. The thriving of a neighborhood begins from within—by mutual care, by recognizing and naming gifts, and by neighbors working to use those gifts to discover how to solve their problems together.

Jesus, wandering through the wilderness with his disciples, comes to a spot on the shore where a great crowd meets him. After he teaches them for a whole day, his disciples point out that everyone is hungry. Jesus responds to them, "Don't look at me. You do something about it."

The disciples are perplexed. What are they to do? They obviously lack what they need to solve the problem. Should they write a grant to the local foundation seeking some funding? Can they find an angel investor interested in hunger issues in this food desert? Would crowdfunding work? They see clearly the pressing issue, but they have no idea how to feed the people. There simply is not enough food. They state the problem with the focus on what is missing from the scene. They feel compelled to look elsewhere for the answer, perhaps in the nearest town. But, even if they went to town, they have no money to buy food. They are paralyzed by their lack. They can only see what is missing.

Jesus, the great community organizer, asks them, "What is here now? What do we have?" He is not interested in what they don't have.

"Teacher, we have five small loaves of bread and two fish from a peasant boy."

They have a riff. Jesus takes their little offering while everyone in the amphitheater watches. All five thousand men, plus women and children, who, it's worth remembering, ought to count also, have their eyes trained on the Teacher. He begins to work off the riff given to him. He is composing on the spot. He sends an idea over to the disciples, asking them to help him. He improvises a song heavenward. And then he invites the crowd to join in their own feeding, using only what they already have. One section of people after another breaks a loaf, shares a fish. They join in the song until everyone is full, and there is yet more food that goes uneaten. From almost nothing, just a little riff of a meal, a banquet is born. Soon they are flourishing, if only for a moment, before heading back into the heat of the Roman occupation. They are thriving from a riff.

The story of the feeding of the five thousand is a narrative about Abundance. With thousands of poor Palestinian peasants gathered together, Jesus brings among them two key ingredients—imagination and power. When the disciples look out at the crowd, they can only imagine a disaster coming. Their imaginations have been formed by Scarcity, a tyrant who insists that there is never enough, that what is needed is always somewhere else. Living in a world where everyone believes in Scarcity (Caesar's house is ruled by it, as are his armies, and his financial advisors, and his business interests) has taken the imaginations of the people gathered, including Jesus's disciples, and deadened them. They can only see what is missing.

It is no surprise that the one who disrupts Scarcity's narrative is a child. He comes forth with a little offering. He still has his imagination, still thinks he can do big things with his little gifts, still believes he can make his dreams come true. There is no wall around his heart yet, and the streets of ancient, occupied Palestine have not yet taken the softness of his spirit. He finds an easy companion in Jesus. And in Jesus, the boy and the crowd have someone who can combine Abundance's imagination with power. Jesus has power, wonder-working power, and at least some of that power is because his imagination is as big as the boy's. Jesus believes that all the people who did not get counted—the wild-eyed children playing on the edges, the wise and weary mamas—have more than can be seen. Among the people are immense gifts ready to be shared.

Now I'm not saying that Jesus did not make food appear out of thin air. If anybody could, it was him. But I know how children operate—little gifts tucked in pockets, gentle spirits ever ready to share. And I've been observing mamas my whole life—raised by one, married to another, nurtured by many others. Those Palestinian mamas didn't just head out for the day, babies in tow, with nothing hidden in their bags. Wonders happen—symphonies are composed!—not just when manna falls from the heavens, but when regular people start putting what they have together to help meet each other's needs. The power that transforms Jesus's words into bread and fish, and his congregation's hunger into a banquet, is the kind of power that believes in abundance, and is willing to give from abundance without fear.

When the shine came off the bank towers in Charlotte, following the release of the Chetty study in 2014 regarding the scarcity of opportunity, municipal and civic leaders in town scrambled to respond. The city has a long history of making policy change in a way that preserves the appearance of good, genteel politics on the outside, while maintaining the same fortress of scarcity on the inside. The initial reaction to the Chetty study was no different. One common denial was that while the study was good, its methodology did not fit well with Charlotte because of the peculiar nature of the place. Others appealed to the city's resolve to work together, an appeal that failed to account for the fact that people had been working together, and economic inequality was still historically bad. Eventually, the formal response was the formation of a "task force," a panel of experts to study the problem and return with recommendations as to courses of action.

Halfway through the task force's study, some public interviews began to appear regarding the process and what the panel was learning. One article, written in March 2016, noted that "some members of the task force found themselves surprised at the wish of some poor families for their children to remain in neighborhood schools and not be bussed to higher-performing schools."[3] Among the panel of experts, it was news that parents in poor neighborhoods wanted to live in better neighborhoods without having to move. That surprise is born from the imagination impoverished by that old tyrant Scarcity. The idea that the good life is accessible only by proximity to the wealthy misses the ways that goodness thrives in places

3. Boschma and Deruy, "Where Children Rarely Escape Poverty."

like Enderly Park, through little riffs of neighborliness. The parents in opportunity deserts saw the possibility already in their neighborhoods. *They were* the possibility already in their neighborhoods. They lived out of the abundant imagination that made their lives possible each day. But they lacked the organized power needed to make important changes for themselves and their children.

Scarcity teaches that making change is the domain of the "expert." Experts come from far-off neighborhoods and towns. They charge fees and receive grants to enter into communities with answers and programs and recommendations, things they gleaned from task forces and boards of inquiry and publications on "best practices." But what is missing from poor neighborhoods is not expertise. Poor people understand their lives—and the reasons they remain poor—perfectly well. What is missing from their lives is power. The power to institute change in suffering places is almost always held by someone who is not poor, someone who belongs outside that place. Government institutions, developers, non-profit organizations, police, doctors, legislators, and even ministers almost all live and locate the power of their institutions elsewhere, on the outside of poor communities. When change is led by experts, who are funded and employed from outside a community, then the change-makers are accountable to someone else, someone other than the people whose lives their work is supposed to affect. This process, enacted by foundations, caseworkers, churches, nonprofits, grantmakers, and task forces, keeps the power and the responsibility for making change outside of those most directly affected by the problems a community experiences.

Communities have within them the assets they need to develop the solutions to their problems. Even the poorest place has a basket of loaves and fish. Organizing people to act on issues that matter to them starts with drawing out the gifts and assets of a community, and binding people together to work and share in building solutions. A community's problems are best solved by the members of the community joining together to work in common, employing experts and outsiders only as needed. As an organizer friend tells me often, "Those closest to the problem are closest to the solution."[4]

---

4. I've learned this—and much more—from amalia deloney, a good friend and brilliant organizer.

The story of the gospels shows Jesus and his band of disciples wandering through the Palestinian countryside, eventually headed toward Jerusalem, the seat of political, economic, and religious power in their region. The last week of his life will be spent there, as the long-brewing conflict between him and the imperial authorities will reach its climax. When the band of castoffs finally make it to the capital, they announce Jesus's curious sort of power by having him enter the city with a performance of street theater. He enters the gates, greeted by throngs of excited people, on a humble donkey rather than a large war horse. He claims to be king, but not in the way common to rulers of his day. He lampoons the whole system by coming in humility proclaiming a different sort of reign.

Jesus's last week on earth keeps moving toward its conclusion when he gathers his followers together for the last time to share a meal. The remembrance of this meal is to become a central moment in all of the Christian theology to follow. This peculiar God, being found in human form, has chosen an odd group of nobodies in an occupied state in a relatively obscure part of the world, and has sat down to eat supper with them. This is strange.

While they are dining together, Jesus takes the most ordinary elements of the meal, bread and wine, and uses them as a riff on which Christian theology is still building. For two millennia, this little improvisation on the elements of a regular meal has been the central act in Christian worship gatherings. Jesus, the host of the meal, takes bread, breaks it, and begins spinning out the meaning of it. The bread is his body, he says. The ordinary loaf, shared with ordinary people, is the body—the form, the being, the substance—of the God who comes to us enfleshed as the peasant king, as one of the despised ones. He hits the blue notes, emphasizing that this will be the last time they eat together until "that great gettin'-up morning." The wine—just a little of it!—is his blood, he tells them. It is the life that flows through the veins of the one whose breath creates and sustains the universe. The existence of everything that is depends on the contents of this cup, and Jesus is offering a share of it with his friends. They will eat and drink of it, and then they will find themselves swallowed up by this life they are taking into their bodies. They eat the meal, but the meal consumes them.

What is happening in that little meal is not the institution of a symbolic world to be contained inside a sanctuary. What is happening is the fracturing of everything thought to be true about the way the world works.

The rupture of the normal order of things will continue to be worked out through the Triduum of Good Friday, Holy Saturday, and Easter Sunday. In the room sits the God of the universe, one sometimes called "omnipotent," possessing all power. This God is using the plain stuff of the world to redistribute power. The illusions of empire, that power is best centralized and wealth is best trickled up, are being shattered in an unremarkable room by a riff on ordinary ingredients. The meal enacts the structure of God's power in the world. That power is given form in sharing, in love that gives itself away for the sake of friends. The depth of one ordinary meal of bread and wine transfigures all of our ordinary meals. The revolution starts at the Table, where the God of creation joins friends and reorients lives back to God and out to one another.

God's dream is as plain as the thriving of family—both blood family and neighborly kinship family—at a banquet. The dream is made manifest in the riff on bread and wine. God's dream persists. Even now, it thrums through veins, this power begging to be given away. And the more it is given, the more powerful it becomes.

The Annunciation of good news, when it comes, is always a blessed surprise, a rift in the world of fear and brokenness we inhabit. The blood will never lose its power, and its power keeps showing up in places we never expect, offering a riff on which to build an improvisation of beauty. At the trap house, while I was looking for Monique, good news came to me in a surprise I never could have expected. "That's not a white man!" Ray only needed a couple of words, and the house party was back on. Before he popped around the corner, all of us were all acting out the drama the world had spelled out long before that night. Ray gave us a new song to sing and a laugh to share. And Anthony went to summer camp, for eight full weeks. He adored it so much that he cried all the way through the closing ceremony, and for an hour after that.

A good riff sticks in the ears. Ray's riff stuck in my ears and buried itself down deep within me. I am still unwrapping what it means, and still questioning whether I am worthy of such a gift. But good gifts are not given only to worthy recipients. This was a gift to keep learning to live into, both an affirmation in the present and a riff with which to keep improvising the world to come.

That's not a white man.

Basie strikes up the band.

KnockKnock.
Do this in remembrance of me.
We are thriving from a riff.

3

Just Friends[1]

Helms and I are with our youth group of one dozen teens at Mars Hill College, a small school in the Blue Ridge Mountains of North Carolina. We have come to join with fifteen other groups for the 2008 edition of summer youth camp. The week promises to be the perfect mix of spiritual growth and teenagers pushing every conceivable limit. There is no reasonable explanation for why otherwise sensible adults continue to put on summer camps. Yet here we are again, for another week of collectively holding our breath. I am partially responsible, having helped to plan the camp and signed the youth up to come. And despite my anxiety, I expect that this week will help to grow some imaginations and to plant some new thoughts in these young people about how they might develop and utilize their gifts.

Following an early wake-up call at home, we drive up hours ahead of registration time in order to hike a spur of the Appalachian Trail called "Lover's Leap." We have picked a beautiful day for the hike. It is dry, a little cool for June, and clear. The trail is perfect. It is short, and becomes steep quickly, almost immediately after the trailhead. Within just a few feet, we already seem to be deep in the forest. The air is different in these woods. It is damp and cool. Sunlight peeks between leaves, dappling the trail under our feet. We are nestled into ancient and wise hills. They offer themselves to us, slowly revealing their rugged charm as we wind higher.

---

1. Parker, "Just Friends." This is the first track from a collection called *Charlie Parker with Strings*, a series of two albums released in 1950 that featured Bird playing with a string orchestra. These records became his biggest sellers, and were admitted to the Grammy Hall of Fame in 1988.

I think these youth catch the difference in the air also, or at least I hope they do. But that in no way slows their obscene amount of complaining. Jarrett knows that we brought him out here to kill him. Crystal is sure that the bears are just behind that tree over there. Camille has to stop every ten steps to rest, and she is just not sure she is going to make it. The youth have all learned the survival skill of turning fear into humor, which means that despite the bellyaching, the trip up is fun.

Our calves are burning, and poor Camille swears she is going to pass out, when the trail flattens out. We have come up the backside of the hill, and now we are cresting it and approaching the overlook. The noise stops. A moment of holiness descends. We survey the French Broad River a thousand feet below us, the river valley giving way to mountains, row after row of hulking shoulders, the sky blue and crisp, holding the impossible together. The moment is brief, but the discovery sparkles in their eyes. How could this place even be here? And can we even believe that we climbed all the way up this mountain?

The moment ends when Camille announces that she could never live here because it would take too long to walk to the corner store.

But the mystery touches us, nestled here in the hills. The mystery still holds us, I remind myself sometimes. We head down to the river to dip our feet in and to commune over sandwiches.

At the end of the first day of camp, we are settling down in the dorm back at the college. The boys and the chaperones take some time to reflect on what we have done over the course of the day. They are all very excited. They tell me about the friends they remember from last summer, the girls they have seen, the basketball competition they have been sizing up, the ice cream included with every meal. Even ice cream for breakfast. We make bets about who will eat the most over the week. We talk until lights out, and then the chaperones double check to be sure that everyone is in their rooms.

I have been a youth minister for long enough—and a youth recently enough—to recall that there are two nights at youth camp where things are most likely to go awry. The last night can be trying for a chaperone, because no one has to give a damn about what the adults say anymore. Everyone is simply riding home the next day, so there is no reasonable punishment to be administered. As a chaperone, there is nothing to do but hope for the best.

The other worrisome night is the first night, when the hormones and energy that always rage through teens have kicked into warp speed. A week of thrills awaits. The freedom of leaving behind families and entering into new turf with hundreds of peers is present. This is no time to sleep. The party must begin.

My first-night-of-camp policy is for chaperones to take up residence in the hallway. We are ready to greet any would-be ruffian or reveler who happens to be slipping through the hall. I grab a journal, a book, and a cold drink, and settle in. Making sure everyone is in bed might take a while, so we are ready. But after half an hour has passed, all seems to be going pretty well. There is not much noise, and while the lights are still on, no one has yet tried so much as dashing across the hall. We are all tired after a long day, and the bed is beginning to call to us. We decide to give it five more minutes when we hear a disturbance in the stairwell. I look up, ready to respond to someone else's youth out making mischief. Instead, towards me marches the dorm's resident director, the only female in the entire residence hall.

She is clearly unhappy. She stops in front of us and points to what I thought, until this moment, was a well-behaved room of my guys. "Who is responsible for these gentlemen?" she asks, pointing to Jake and Shawn's room. "I'm directly under them, and it sounds like a drumline rehearsal in there."

"I am," I answer. "But we have been sitting a couple of feet from their door for nearly an hour now, and we haven't noticed any noise."

I am legitimately curious, ready to defend my youth but also ready to establish to them from the first day what my expectations are and exactly how I want them met. She insists that Jake and Shawn's room is the guilty one, so I make my decision. These boys are going to know that I am in charge and that I expect full compliance when it comes to bedtime habits. Roused from my reverie, I puff out my chest, hike up my pants, lower my voice, and pound on the door, ready to set the tone for an orderly, well-behaved week.

"Fellows, what's going on in here? This poor lady is complaining about the noise she hears from your room. She says y'all are louder than a herd of elephants."

Shawn and Jake look innocent enough. They are in bed, and seem not just a little surprised that I am questioning them. They deny causing any noise. "We're just laying here, Greg," Shawn says.

At first glance, I think that maybe the resident director is imagining things. Nothing appears unusual. The guys are quiet, and I know them well enough to sense that they are telling me the truth. This is a tight spot for me—who am I going to side with? The angry Resident Director, who is in charge and able to make complaints to our camp leadership? My young men, who are trying to make it this week in a world far from home in almost every way, and who are trusting me to keep them safe? Or my own gut, which senses that something is not right about the accusation, but also needs to set clear boundaries?

A second look around the room reveals where the noise has come from. Shawn and Jake decided to do some redecorating in their dorm room. They rearranged the furniture. The desks are piled in one corner, the wardrobes in another, and the beds are shoved together in the leftover space. This strikes me as odd. Shawn and Jake grew up on one of the toughest streets in Charlotte. At fifteen or sixteen years old, they have cultivated a correspondingly tough image. And as straight teenage boys, I suspect that the intimacy of sleeping so close together might be a bit uncomfortable for them.

The noise complaint makes sense now. The sound of furniture being pushed across their floor, which was the resident director's ceiling, created a lot of racket. I'm not upset at this point, just curious, and I am absolutely going to side with my guys. So I ask why they have redecorated the room.

Shawn jumps to explain. "Now, Greg, don't get mad about that. It's just that Jake forgot his blanket, so I told him that we could push our beds together and I would share mine."

The friendships that I witness and am a part of in Enderly Park are part of the story of my salvation. They are the clearest way that the good news is at work in my life. Jesus calls in gentle and surprising ways that move me to deeper love of God and neighbor. Jake and Shawn are two friends who witness to God's tender love for all creation.

As I pound on their door the first night of camp, I am ready to be a teacher and disciplinarian. I am prepared to assert my leadership and to show Jake and Shawn the error of their ways. To me, the most important thing about the experience of this first night is the establishment of a hierarchy, the clear communication that my trust of them will be built on their willingness to do what I say. They are being rude, I plan to say. They are not following my instructions.

But my priorities for them are not their own priorities. They have other work to do, the kind that Jesus describes in the Sermon on the Mount when he teaches his hearers not to do their good works in public, looking for affirmation. Instead, do them in secret, without seeking recognition. I suspect that Shawn has practiced this way of goodness for so long that it never occurrs to him to do anything else. Shawn does not talk much about Jesus, but he lives in a way that shows deep theological knowledge alive in his body.

I knock on Shawn and Jake's door unaware that I am entering sacred ground that will train me into the meaning and practice of friendship. This will not be a class in friendship as an idea. There will be no philosophical theory of friendship. It is far more personal than that. Jake and Shawn are teaching me what kind of friend I am, and what kind of friend I could learn to be.

I am learning that I am the kind of friend that, had Jake told me about his lack of covers, would have responded immediately. But my response would have been based out of pity for him, and a chance to be a hero for myself. I would have seen him as a charity case, and would have gone out quickly to buy some stuff for him. I believe in Visa as my Lord and Savior, Wal-Mart as the manifestation of God's abundance on the earth. The following morning I would have acted a little tired so that I could quietly tell a couple of other chaperones about my midnight run. I would have pretended not to make a big deal out of it while not keeping it totally secret.

Having a friend who can and will buy you a blanket when you need a blanket is not without value. A good friend will want to do that for you if they can. In a one-time situation, having a relationship where you can confide a need to someone who is willing to utilize their own resources to help is a beautiful thing. Everyone needs to be in relationships like that, on both the side of giving and the side of need.

But that is not what is happening here. Jake does not confide in me. In fact, he chooses not to. Perhaps he knows I will turn him into a charity case. Perhaps he senses that I cannot be fully trusted with such sensitive information about his lack of resources. Maybe he just does not think about it, because a lack of resources has always been the norm for him. In a situation where he lacks what he needs, he uses what he has—a friend. He confides in Shawn with the trust that their growing up together has created a solidarity whereby Shawn will take Jake's problem and turn it into his own, at which point the two of them can work together to solve the problem.

This is the kind of friendship on display at Mars Hill College on this night. Those young men lie down together in solidarity, where the problem of one becomes the problem of both. Theirs is the kind of friendship that Jesus, the enfleshed God who "moves to the neighborhood,"[2] embodies in the gospel. Jake and Shawn are preaching the good news to me with their lives.

⤙

A few years after that trip to youth camp, a musical friendship landed me in Cuba for a week to play saxophone and to join in a longstanding series of cross-church friendships. Our group of three men and two women lodged in the guest space of Primera Iglesia Bautista—First Baptist Church—of Matanzas, Cuba. Matanzas is the birthplace of the rhumba, the sensual dance that informs pop music around the world. The city still breathes the rhythms of delight, which you can hear in the liveliness of its sidewalks and squares. Street theater regularly takes over public plazas, adding visual drama to the sounds of the city. Concerts are regular events, sometimes in beautiful halls on weekday afternoons, sometimes in the open air on weekends, always with every seat filled. The architecture astonishes. Behind a crumbling facade is a portico featuring artisan tile work. An art gallery without a roof becomes a living museum piece blurring the lines between indoors and outdoors, between the natural world and the built one.

Cuban cuisine is tasty, though quite simple. Each morning, we have boiled eggs, bread, and butter for our breakfast. But one morning, we do not have eggs to add to our morning meal of bread and butter, juice, and coffee. By chance, the particular day is Fat Tuesday, or Mardi Gras, or Carnival. This is the most well-known feast day on the church calendar. It marks the day before Ash Wednesday, the beginning of the season of fasting and self-denial called Lent. Across much of the world, communities celebrate with feasting and parades. Bakers are mixing mountains of sugar, butter, and flour. Marchers are prepping costumes exploding with color for parades and extravaganzas. Trumpeters are warming up their lips and their horns. Drummers are tuning the heads on their drums and tending the calluses on their hands. The day promises to be a wild feast for eyes and ears and mouths. Except in Matanzas, where Ash Wednesday has come a day early.

2. John 1:14 (The Message Bible).

I try to connect with the cook at the church, who is obviously embarrassed that the already plain morning routine has gotten simplified down even further.

"It's no problem," I say, hacking her native language to pieces in the process. "Sometimes I forget something on the grocery list as well."

She smiles in a way that makes me suspect I do not understand the problem. Forgetfulness may not be the issue for our hosts this morning. It could be that there is an egg shortage right now, which is to say that not only do we not have eggs, but a whole bunch of other people are taking their breakfast *sin huevos* this morning also. This is not uncommon in Matanzas, where lines at the market for basic necessities are a regular feature of life and shortages are pretty normal. Perhaps she just forgot, but it seems likely enough that there may not have been any eggs. Who knows?

Whatever the case, I decide that this very simple breakfast is chance to move into an imaginative space where I can, at least for a moment, consider this fast as one not by choice or forgetfulness, but by necessity. On this last feast day before forty days of fasting, I will make the momentary lack of an important resource into a small step into solidarity with the brothers and sisters here, and back in my own neighborhood, for whom eggs are not the only thing in short supply. While much of the rest of the world gorges itself, I will try to remember that celebrations never reach full consummation when some brothers and sisters never have a full-on feast. What if I carry with me that the constant feast that is American life is at least one of the factors in the unchosen daily fasting that is the norm around the world? What if such solidarity were a regular characteristic of my discipleship in Enderly Park?

Over the course of a week of visits with Cuban churches, artists, and musicians, I heard often about solidarity. In a land of both tremendous beauty and crumbling infrastructure, a land of the sensual rhumba and of hardscrabble subsistence, our group connected with people who refused to leave their homeland, even when they had the option. Their work, their bodies, their whole lives were given as offerings towards the building of their communities. Church folks we met with described staying as an act of faith. It was also a triumph of imagination. The ability to see possibility amid suffering takes faith, vision, imagination, and a large portion of courage. There certainly have been days when the people of Matanzas lacked more than eggs, and yet they have carved out spaces of beauty and solidarity, of creative resistance and abundant life.

Christians in the United States lack the same sense of regular, daily solidarity with one another. I needed no reminder of this, but I got one on the way home. After a week away from the internet or the telephone, I turned on my mobile phone to call home when I arrived in the Miami airport. The phone call with my children was a delight, but I saw quickly that turning my phone on may have been a mistake. Automatically, a deluge of email and notifications began buzzing in my ears. Among the flood of communication in my inbox was a grant application that had arrived, by chance, on that eggless Fat Tuesday. It came from a very wealthy church across town. They annually distribute a portion of their budget to organizations working for justice in the community. QC Family Tree has often been a recipient of some of those funds. Sitting near a gate waiting on my next flight, I saw that the application this year was accompanied by a new disclaimer, which read, "Please be aware that our funds are very limited for this grant cycle."

An airport is a kind of no-place, a space that exists as a means of getting somewhere else. I am between two worlds—supposedly in Miami, really stuck between Matanzas and Charlotte. The rhumba is echoing in my head. Only a few hours prior, I was in Leo's art gallery. He had taken an old building near to falling down and turned it into a sculpture studio. The roof was gone over most of the building. Lacking money, but rich in imagination, he decided to work from an open air studio. With the front door looking over the Rio San Juan, he was creating sculptures with subtle and subversive political and religious themes. His work had earned him recognition around the world. The neighborhood rallied around his work, turning his space into a place for conversation and for building connections, a sort of public commons energized by his imagination.

At the same time I am remembering Leo's studio, I can conjure an image of a Charlotte church "with very limited funds," but with a tall steeple shading a parking lot full of BMWs. They have endowments and trust funds and the air of self-importance. The doors are all ten feet tall with heavy, museum-piece knobs, for viewing rather than turning, and dentil moulding decorating their casings. Each window has a proper architrave on top. A slate tile roof covers the entire building.

Sitting in Miami, suspended between two worlds, I see that the places I hang in between are immeasurably far apart. In the one where I have been, I have witnessed friendships built on a disposition of abundance, despite the conditions of scarcity. Resources are few, but there is enough time to stop work and share a pot of coffee. There are enough found objects to make something ordinary into something beautiful.

In the other world, the one I am returning to, I will be engaging in relationships built on scarcity, despite the conspicuous display of abundance. There are so many resources that the wealthy church needs managers just for their money. They say "Our funds are very limited during this cycle" because the excess of things and money, the overwhelming wealth, makes the illusion of scarcity seem real. This is a deep contradiction in the way of the world—those with too much believing there is not enough, and those with too little giving from deep abundance.

How curious (and yet, how normal), that a church, the gathered people of God, would believe that there is not enough, especially in a place of conspicuous wealth. Abundance, in Christian theology, is built into the foundations of the universe. God exists as an abundance, so overflowing in goodness that God can only be described as mathematical nonsense—three-in-one and one-in-three. Out of this abundance, God improvises something new, a creation of land and people, of persimmons and snow leopards, of sweet gum trees and sand dunes. God creates it all for friendship, between people and the land that sustains them, between God and people, between God and the peculiar creation that flows out of God's extravagant existence. In this world of bounty, there is enough—enough stuff to care for every neighbor, enough time to make enemies into friends, enough imagination to re-envision the world.

The closest God comes to scarcity is in Jesus's self-emptying on the cross, suffering to the point of death. But even self-emptying creates another opportunity for the display of God's abundance. God chooses to work in the world through the kind of friendship that looks like self-emptying, yet becomes a display of abundant life. Jesus appears in solidarity with those who bear flesh, who face the limitations of cold and hunger and desire and disease. The God-become-human shows that by emptying oneself, a new path of overflowing creativity is born.

⟜

Anyone who has ever worked on a significant project with a partner or a group knows the feeling of adrenaline that rushes through the body as a plan comes into action. Whether building a house, or starting a business, or working on a campaign, beginning to bring vision to reality is an exhilarating time. What is even more exciting is the way that mutuality in work binds people together. The bonds formed out of shared labor hold people deeply. The best fruit of labor together is not the product, it is the community that develops through the work. A common labor or project simply gives people a reason to be together in the formation of a community.

This is the mystery of faith—doing one thing produces something else even better. The Eucharist is not about eating. Baptism is not about going for a swim. The sacraments are communal acts that seal the bonds of participants by producing communities that can act in the world the way they act during liturgies—with solidarity, with careful attention to the needs of each member, without fear of strangers.

In the sixth century BCE, the people of Israel endured their greatest national crisis. The cruel army from Babylon attacked their capital Jerusalem, destroyed all of their sacred sites, ransacked and burned the city, and then took those with religious, cultural, and political power into exile, far away from home. Israel spent fifty years under Babylonian rule and another thirty under Persian rule, following the fall of Babylon. Finally, the weight of their oppression began to lift when the exiles were released to go home and start rebuilding their beloved capital. The Persian King Cyrus even sent them with a blank check to jumpstart the rebuilding. As an emperor, Cyrus practiced an enlightened self-interest. He knew that happy subjects resisted less and paid taxes more frequently.

The leader of the rebuilding effort was Nehemiah, for whom a book of the Hebrew Bible is named. Nehemiah did a remarkable job of convincing everyone who was returning, regardless of their level of wealth or their position of power within the society, that it was in everyone's best interest to rebuild Jerusalem's crumbled walls together. Nehemiah's most important job was to get them organized, so that the people were in the right place, the money needed was available, and the job got done. Everyone joined in the effort, with each person doing what they were able. The wall was part of the common wealth of Jerusalem, so all the residents got involved. The wall protected everyone from raids by barbarians and roaming pariahs. A strong wall was a benefit to every citizen and guest. Likewise, a breached wall endangered all. So, in a remarkable feat of collective will, all the residents of Jerusalem took a role in its reconstruction. When nearby enemies began to threaten them, they added patrols and watchmen to the list of common work that needed to be done in the revitalization of Jerusalem.

This manner of working together persisted for a while, but then things took a wrong turn. Nehemiah had organized the whole community to work together on a massive public works project designed to serve everyone. For a while, everyone was working, but then some decided that they would not do labor anymore. They would be bankers instead. And so, they began to offer loans and mortgages to people who needed cash. Groceries were expensive, and building the wall, while serving the public good, limited some people's earnings potential. A select few of the well-capitalized began making money available. Since the need was stark and immediate—people were unable to eat—the new bankers were able to set terms that were advantageous to themselves. They would provide cash, but the collateral on the loan was some combination of house, farm, vineyard, and children. Faced with starvation, the common laborers had little choice. They signed the paperwork and prayed they would be able to work it out. Predictably, the day came quickly when they could not make the payments, and so their daughters were sold into slavery. Their livelihoods were repossessed. Their ancestral vineyards were confiscated. They cried out for help to Nehemiah. The people said, "Our lives matter." Their pain was acute and it needed to be addressed immediately.

I was telling this story to our youth group during a youth meeting, and I asked them what they thought Nehemiah, the leader of the people, would do. Most of them figured he would do nothing. The youth suspected this because they have lived with their necks under the boots of leaders and governing councils all their lives. Whether they can fully express it or not, those wise youth see that governmental and financial systems are very efficient at serving the interests of the powerful at the expense of kids who grow up in opportunity deserts, who are vulnerable to the whims of the wealthy. Power tends to work in those who have it by breaking the bonds of solidarity that otherwise would unite neighbors in mutual care. For our youth, it has become clear from their earliest consciousness that as people of color, they do not hold the position of power in American culture, and that they cannot expect the powerful to treat them with fairness and dignity.

Layla has a gift for perception. She recognizes that the answer to the question of what Nehemiah is likely to do is somewhat more complex than "nothing."

"He is going to say he will help, but then not do anything," she answers.

This too is a common course of action. Layla knows this. She has seen it. She has heard, even at 12 years old, powerful people who say the right thing, or who say what they think they should say, but have little intention of acting. She also understands that some folks have the right intentions, but find action to be too difficult. People mean well, but then they get involved in the struggle and find out that the work is hard and the laborers are few. Sometimes workers show up and get scared because they learn that they are implicated in the problem. This can make the pain of acting too great to continue. Freedom can have too high a price to pay for those who benefit from unearned privilege.

I imagine yet another response. When the people cry out, "Our lives matter," their oppressors respond, "No, all lives matter." This is a strategy to keep distance from the pain that is acutely felt in some places by pretending that it does not exist. It is true that every life in Nehemiah's story mattered, but not all of the lives were being sold into slavery to pay unfair debts. Not every family was having their ancestral homes taken from them for unjust gain by others. Attending to the pain of those who were hurting most acutely by dismissing them highlights how deeply the solidarity born of abundance had been ruptured.

For Nehemiah's people, seeing their interrelation with those who are crying out does not even require much in the way of imagination. The folks who are using financial instruments to take vineyards and daughters as collateral are living next door to those whose vineyards and daughters they are taking. They are watching their neighbors build the wall day and night for the benefit of all. Yet somehow, they are able to ignore the cries of those who are working on their behalf. Their hearts have been hardened—emerging from their recent captivity in Babylon, some of the Israelite people imagine themselves back into captivity again. They become a Nebuchadnezzar unto themselves.

The practice of taking one's neighbor's property or children as collateral went on long enough that it was not merely an isolated event. Rather, it became like a system—a series of coordinated components that led to a particular outcome. Pressed for their basic needs because of their labor on a public works project, a family would go in search of assistance. They had few options to meet immediate needs, and so would take a loan at the high risk of not being able to pay it back. The lenders appeared to be working together to offer similar terms on the loans they made. Options were limited. Goods were scarce. Families did what they had to do. The practice of neighborly care was being done not by neighbors with one another, but by those coordinated components of a system created to guarantee a particular outcome. In this case, it destroyed neighborliness. The outcome was harmful to everyone, but the most immediate and acute harm happened to those whose families and livelihoods were at stake.

The financial system created in the story was oppressive, meaning it placed some people within the story at significant and long-lasting disadvantage in ways beyond their control. At the same time, the system advantaged another group within the story, the money-lenders, who enriched themselves from their neighbors' troubles. The pain of this financial system became too great for those suffering from it, and so those who were losing their land and their families cried out. They protested their unfair treatment to Nehemiah.

This is where the story surprised Layla and me. The protest reached Nehemiah's house, and he heard the protesters. He believed them. He took them seriously, listened to the ways their families were distraught, and he was moved to act. Nehemiah confronted the financial elites who were oppressing the poor by their unfair lending practices, and by their refusal to participate in the building of Jerusalem's common wealth. Nehemiah not only confronted the oppressors, he confronted the oppressor in himself. He confessed to his own role as one of the unjust money lenders, and made a promise to change things. And then he took the most courageous step possible. He demanded repentance and corrective action from himself and from his colleagues who were engaged in the oppression with him. He insisted on reparations—goods being returned, restitutions being paid, relationships healed. He put an end to a system that privileged some lives at the expense of others, and fixed the damage it had done.

The surprises continued. Nehemiah confessed his own sin. He named the brokenness of the system that the privileged created, and insisted on repairing the damage done. And those who were upholding that system agreed—their oppression of their brothers and sisters was wrong. They decided to turn away from the direction they had chosen, and instead to meet the demands for repentance and repair. They got to work fixing the damage they had done to their neighbors and their city, returning land and children to the people they rightly belonged to. This moment of healing in Jerusalem did not last long before other temptations crept in, and other divisions with other neighbors formed. But for at least a brief time, the imagination of the people about the possibility of life together in neighborly solidarity was sparked, and they began to heal their divisions, and to learn to live together as friends.

Aristotle claimed that "If people are friends, they have no need of justice." Friendships will carve out spaces that are built around rightness and equity. Friends may still hurt one another, but friendships make repairing harm easier. The bond of affection, and the proximity of friends to one another, will make the pain of broken trust, or harmful words or actions, the problem of both people in the relationship. To be a friend is to understand belonging to one another, and to let someone else's hurt become your problem also. Friendships motivate people to act.

Friendships will create spaces of justice and rightness between people. But having a friend, or even lots of friends, will not stop the injustice of the world from harming loved ones. Living in Enderly Park has forced me to see ongoing injustices that I would not have seen living elsewhere, and has given me an expanded imagination about how to respond. Walking with people through the legal system, with police and courts and jails, presents one set of opportunities for friends to act together, for themselves and for one another. Part of the work I do with QC Family Tree is around housing. Seeing the struggles that neighbors have in accessing and maintaining affordable, welcoming, and culturally comfortable neighborhoods has led me to act on housing issues. Seeing children in separate and unequal schools, and knowing the names of children being underserved in those schools, and the names of teachers who are doing their best in under-resourced places, means being willing to advocate for different policies, and to spend time as a volunteer working for better outcomes for students. Friendship is a place to start in the work for justice. But friendship in a complex society is not enough. My friends needs justice.

I learn one Friday night how friendship can create the kind of imagination that helps in facing injustice in new ways, and to create new systems that embody justice for all of the friends of God. On this Friday, only a couple of months after moving to Enderly Park, the living room of the hospitality house is filled with teens. The adults are playing cards with the young people, not because we like cards that much, but because we like being together. The cool fall air has brought us in off the porch, but we can still hear the drum line at the high school football game just down the road. The hour is growing late when two of our favorite young men come dashing in. Marcus and Will were out walking and heard gunshots near them, so they ran to the nearest safe place they know. They recount the whole experience to us—shots, voices, their run to the house. We laugh together because their narration is funny. Humor hedges against terror. But their insides are roiling and ours are too. Everyone in the room knows that this is neither the first time nor the last time that we will have this feeling, knowing that a life can vanish at any time, that our love for one another cannot prevent the streets from snuffing out a bright light.

We begin to settle back in and start a new game when we note the drone of a helicopter above. The police are out searching for a suspect. We can hear that they are looking close by, aided by a few cruisers riding down the street. We are grateful to be inside, safe and together.

But then, an officer and his partner walk onto our porch. I greet them at the door, and see that there are three others running down our driveway. There are two more in the front yard to the left. Three near the pecan tree by the street. Two cruisers parked on the side street. And the helicopter is not just close by, it is circling above our house. We are surrounded.

"We are looking for two Black males, one shorter than the other, wearing dark clothes," the officer says. "Two that match that description were seen entering your house a few moments ago."

The description is a shot in the dark, but I'm too new to understand that this is how things work in Enderly Park, and in any neighborhood where people "live with their backs constantly against the wall."[3] The description fits basically every pair of Black males on the street tonight, or any night. I explain that the two young men who just entered my house were looking for the same safety that we all desire when someone is shooting a gun close by. We discuss, to the extent that you *can* discuss anything when the other side is fortified by a dozen armed men and a helicopter droning overhead. So, the course of action is given to us. The victim of an attempted carjacking is one block over in a patrol car. The two young men are to walk out onto our porch, and an officer will drive the victim by, stopping to shine a blinding spotlight mounted on his car onto our young men. The victim will either positively or negatively identify the fellows. We are surrounded, we are nervous, and we do not know what to do. We intuit this is risky, but Marcus and Will, portraying confidence in themselves and their innocence, head out the door.

---

3. Thurman, *Jesus and the Disinherited*, 3.

This is what you do when the weight of a system designed to crush people you love is bearing down on your friends, blinding them in a white gaze: you stand next to them. You become suspects in the lineup. When they roll by and shine the spot on them, you keep your eyes open. When you still see the light hours later because it has seared your retina, you hold onto that vision. The scales start to fall off your eyes as you see the first glimpses of what it means to live with those whose backs are against the wall. Your conversion is deepening while the chopper hovers above the house on your Damascus Road.

When the call comes that these are not the guys, your legs tremble. Your relief is tempered by cold reality—it is not hard to see that having a burning, blinding spotlight aimed at them is not new for your friends. You sense that the "hounds of hell"[4] will always be nipping at their heels. And you know that while standing next to one another or holding hands or praying is all you can do sometimes, and that sometimes it even works, the day is coming when it will not be enough.

Marcus and Will live in a culture that has not fundamentally changed since its founding. They inhabit a space nearly identical to James Baldwin's Harlem, a world whose pressures lead him to warn his nephew that, "this . . . country set you down in a ghetto in which, in fact, it intended you should perish."[5] In every institution that Marcus and Will encounter—whether school, or court, or bank, or real estate agency, or police department—their lives are valued less than my life is. It is right to state this using the economic term "value." Racism is an economic strategy that uses melanin as a marker for power, a reason to plunder the bodies, the work, the land of some rather than others. The concentration of melanin in epidermis is seen as a justifying factor in the concentration of poverty in neighborhoods and the concentration of neighbors in prisons and jails. Marcus and Will were born into a place where false gods pre-ordained that they would stand repeatedly under blinding white fires until they could be positively identified as what white American culture from its foundations has determined them to be—guilty, worthless, predatory, violent. Everything but a child of God.

Marcus and Will need justice—that is, they need a society organized around full equity, that offers to them every opportunity afforded to me or to anyone else. Having robust friendships will not guarantee justice, but

4. Ibid., 26.
5. Baldwin, *The Fire Next Time*, 7.

without friendships, justice will be impossible. The small move of learning to know a neighbor as a friend, to see them as something besides an Other, whose body is to be controlled and ghettoized and warehoused in undesirable places, is an important start. But that small move is hardly a robust conception of justice. Justice is necessarily social—there is no other kind. It must extend beyond private relationships. More than friendship is needed, but friendship will push people to work together for justice.

Among the things friends do when they gather, in groups of two or three or more, is to sing. Joining voices in song is a physical means of joining bodies together to work in harmony and solidarity with one another. A song in duet, or trio, or in a chorus, is a rehearsal of a social order built on solidarity and belonging. Everyone gets a part. Every part matters. Singing together prefigures the coming world, the world of equity and rightness, of creative dissonances and moments of resolution. This is why worship services often end with song, before the congregation goes out to serve the world, or why protest movements include singing and chanting in the streets.

Children learn to sing by matching their voices with their parents. Jesus learned to sing from Mary and Joseph, probably many kinds of songs. Silly ones. Lullabies. Songs for learning letters and numbers. One of those songs is still around. Mary started singing it from the first moments when she learned that the justice of God was living in her womb. The vibrations of her song were already working through him then. She must have kept singing that song to him as she told him the story of their people, and how their people's God

> has scattered the proud in the thoughts of their hearts.
> He has brought down the powerful from their thrones,
>   and lifted up the lowly;
> he has filled the hungry with good things,
>   and sent the rich away empty.
> He has helped his servant Israel,
>   In remembrance of his mercy,
> According to the promise he made to our ancestors,
>   To Abraham and to his descendants forever.[6]

This is the justice that friends will work together for, and pray together for, and stand together for. It brings down the powerful and lifts up the

6. Luke 1:51b–53.

lowly, creating from a song the kinds of spaces where all of God's children can thrive.

4

Alabama[1]

Remembering that it happened once,
We cannot turn away the thought,
As we go out, cold, to our barns,
Towards the long night's end, that we
Ourselves are living in the world
It happened in when it first happened.[2]

AN ENERGETIC OLD MAN gets out of his truck one afternoon and walks up to Helms in the front yard. She is spreading mulch with some helpers when he approaches. "Pardon me," he says, in his silky smooth voice. "I need to let you know that I have been driving by this house on a regular basis, and I can tell in my spirit that there is something good happening here." He places his hands on her shoulders in a way that shows gentle authority and begins to speak. "I want to say thank you. I'd like to offer you a blessing from the elders, because I can see that you are building what we called back in the movement the 'Beloved Community.'"

And with that, he gets back in his pickup and drives away. Helms reports this to me with a sense of awe right after it happens. This is the sort of interaction that could be strange or uncomfortable in most scenarios—an unknown man touching her and offering some cryptic words about how he has been watching from a distance. She senses that this was different in

1. Coltrane, "Alabama."
2. Berry, *A Timbered Choir*, 94.

some way. His authenticity and authority were genuine in a way that she cannot explain. But the mystery remains. Who is this man?

Only a few days later, Helms is with some youth in Charlotte's history museum when she spots him again, this time in a video presentation on the civil rights struggle in our city. He is Charles Jones, original member of the Student Nonviolent Coordinating Committee, leader of the student movement in Charlotte, and Freedom Rider in the summer of 1961. He is not some strange old man. He is an Elder, a source of wisdom whose words deserve our attention and whose journey is to be revered. And improbably, he decides to become our friend.

Charles begins to make a habit of stopping in to visit and tell stories. Every visit is a moment of serendipity. Whatever we are doing stops, no matter how important it seems, as he struts in and settles on the couch. We hear about an adventure of his, or some trouble he got into, or about a friend whose name we know from history books.

The drama of one of Charles's visits has a regular pattern. He pulls up. We quickly hide the clutter of the house while he slowly gets himself from the car and up the walk. Charles moves with a little limp, the result of 75 years of living and some time on the chain gang. He wears the limp well. I suspect that it is not an unfortunate effect of arthritis or bursitis. In his world, it is not some source of complaint, like a guest who outstayed his welcome. No, the limp is lucky to have him. Charles turns the landscape upside down in that way.

Moving together, Charles and the limp, his walk is a dance. It is a hint that there is music in his head. The music does not stay in his head, but becomes a regular part of his speech. He starts singing whenever the spirit strikes him, as though he lives in a Broadway musical. Song just bursts forth, or even rap. Every person he meets gets a personalized song as a first-time greeting—"Hello, Lou-ee, we've got work to do-ee, and I'm glad to beeee, here with you, you seeeeee. Hey!" He strikes a pose to finish. I swear I am not making this up.

You notice, when it is your turn to receive a song, that he is really looking into your eyes while he sings. He speaks a word about what he sees in your spirit—your gentleness, or your fierceness, or your kindness, or your love. He pays attention in that way. And when an Elder speaks to you in such a fashion, you know that there is truth, even if you have not recognized it yet. This is enchanting to children, who have not been hardened like adults into distrusting his routine. But even for adults, who are suspicious from the start, the song and dance routine melts their resistance. Charles really sees you, and he is patient in showing that to you.

During the summer of 2015, our youth group decides that our annual summer trip is going to take us across the South. We will follow the path of the Freedom Riders. These were the brave young people who decided to test interstate commerce laws by riding commercial buses through the South. In May of 1961, the first groups of Freedom Riders boarded Greyhounds in Washington DC, in mixed racial groups, leaving for New Orleans. A 1960 Supreme Court case, on the basis of the Constitution's interstate commerce clause, had ordered an end to the federal government's non-enforcement of a restriction against segregated bus terminals. Their historic journey tested whether the Court's ruling would be followed. If it was, then public accommodations for interstate travel would be open and accessible to persons of any race, and the riders would arrive unharmed and unbothered in New Orleans. Predictably, this is not what happened. The trip nearly cost some of the participants their lives.

In preparation for our journey, we plan and study for weeks. We learn lots of history of the Civil Rights movement, especially of those places where we will stop along the way. Our youth begin to make connections about how that history remains alive in our own time. We even march, joining the Moral Monday movement in North Carolina for a large demonstration. The subject of our march is voting rights. The North Carolina General Assembly, the state legislative branch, has passed the nation's most extreme set of voting restrictions. Those restrictions were later ruled to have been enacted, according to the U.S. Circuit Court of Appeals, "with almost surgical precision" for the purpose of disenfranchising minority voters. The legislative action would disproportionately affect people just like our youth and their parents. Such attacks, we are coming to see, are a regular feature of American history. Each time reformers make progress toward a more perfect union, there is a predictable backlash that seeks to erase that progress. We understand that our learning is not for the sake of learning alone. It is because we are becoming part of the movement, joining those voices who throughout history have sung songs and taken to the streets in love and anger.

The work our youth are doing is not new. They stand in a tradition of people who were willing to take risks to proclaim a different, more beautiful vision of how humans can live together. The risks we take are less acute than those of Charles and the Freedom Riders. No one is going to attack us at a gas station as we stop along the way. But chaperones, youth, and parents all feel a sense that what we are doing is unusual. And more than one parent expresses concerns about driving Black children across Alabama and Mississippi. In a time of tensions raised by the police killings of unarmed Black people, the memory of historical traumas is working into the way we are thinking about this trip. The tradition of the elders cautioned people not to embark on an important journey without preparation. To prepare ourselves for this journey across the South, we know we need to hear from an Elder who can help us to understand and can offer a blessing before our journey. We call on Charles, who is delighted to come and speak.

Charles arrives as usual. He takes twenty minutes to get from front door to seat, with fifteen songs along the way. He brings along a few tokens to show us—copies of mug shots from his experiences organizing for racial justice in southwest Georgia, for instance, or a clipping from a newspaper detailing an action he planned. Charles was there when it first happened. He greeted the Freedom Riders in Charlotte, when they stayed overnight here. Following his spring semester exams, he met up with them in Montgomery to continue the ride. He captivates us all, talking about his fear, his resolve, and about the sense of joy that the group experienced together in spite of the troubles visited upon them. The youth are rapt, sitting literally at the feet of this Elder, who looks into their eyes and offers his blessing to each one, by name, for the journey they are embarking upon.

Adding to the excitement, our local paper has sent a reporter and a photographer to document this. We are not just talking about history, our youth are saying. We are living it, and we are sharing with those who lived it before us. Alicia, one of the youth participants, perfectly sums up the in-between times we live in, and the nature of our journey: "It's not the same, but it's not different."[3]

When the Freedom Riders rode southward in 1961, they ran into their first major trouble in Anniston, Alabama. A mob met them at the bus station and chased them out of town, slashing the bus's tires as they pulled away. When the bus could go no further because of the flats, it was set on fire by a mob of angry white people. Riders were forced out of a burning bus into the vicious crowd. A number were beaten badly.

3. Link to story: http://www.charlotteobserver.com/news/local/article28702810.html.

We recount this story as we eat our lunch in a park near the old bus station in Anniston on the second day of our Freedom Ride journey. We are only a block away from the bus station Charles's friends had to flee fifty-four years prior. The message of that day was that the Freedom Riders were not welcome in Anniston. The messaging has not changed since then, though the delivery has. Now the architecture speaks. An old industrial building is growing trees through the roof and vines out the window. Storefronts have sagging doorframes that no human has passed through for years. There are sidewalks, but no people. After lunch, we bag up our waste and take it with us because the trash cans are a week beyond capacity. Anniston still bears the burden of the historical traumas that live there. The new messaging says that white folks would prefer to abandon the city rather than to integrate it.

There is one new building, though. It is a jail, euphemistically called a "justice center," sitting directly across from the park. The sidewalk is clean in front of the jail, while the playground is strewn with litter. Jim Crow is gone, but James Crow, Esquire, is building infrastructure. Separate and unequal persists. Now architecture speaks what polite people dare not say.

Following lunch, we keep moving toward Birmingham, our imaginations opening further to what it could have been like to be chased out of town with no knowledge of where the next safe place might be. The youth keep noticing that the most common iconography they see through the van window is the Confederate flag. This narrows the distance between them in 2015 and Charles and his friends in 1961 considerably. The bodies of the youth know the same old fear the Elders had traveled with decades ago. They feel it in their bones. The fear escapes through a muffled shout or a grunt of despair when they see the "stars and bars" yet again. It stands defiant outside businesses, in front of homes, on billboards.

"Why?" they ask, knowing there is no answer good enough. The heritage of hate lives on as the Lost Cause continues to infect land and minds. The flag does us the service of marking places as unsafe. We know where not to stop. But its regular presence disturbs the peace of our highway fellowship. There is comfort in being together, but we are far, far from home. I cannot feel the same fear my youth feel, because my body is not in the same jeopardy theirs is in. And my body does not hold the historical memory of the time, not that long ago, when that jeopardy was even more acute. But I do notice myself growing more tense as we travel deeper into the South. On the rural roads we drive through Alabama and Mississippi, the anxiety in the van thickens. Our vans have seemed trustworthy so far, but one never knows what could happen. We see roadside markers of a lynching here, or an uprising violently put down there. Cell phone service at times becomes weak. We are often far from cities and towns, praying that our radiators will survive August in Mississippi.

Again, the imaginative distance between us and Charles shrinks. The distance between me, the driver, and my beloved passengers shrinks also. Their fear is not mine. I cannot know what it is to live in their skin. And yet, because I love them, and because they love me, to witness their fear in close proximity to their bodies—and even to bear responsibility for the safety of their bodies and their spirits—means that my imagination can grow beyond what it was. Love does that. It helps us to imagine the details of a beloved's life as we could not imagine without love. It rips away the blinders that keep us from seeing the other in their fullness. Love puts our bodies next to the bodies of our neighbors, so that what is foreign to our experience can begin to seep into us. You can feel it in the surge of your pulse when faced with a potential menace. The name for the clenching of your gut when a deep fear arises is love. That fear may be remote, maybe even imagined, but the feeling in your body is real. It remains an approximation of what your neighbor feels, which you cannot know in full. But imaginative love reduces the distance.

In Birmingham, our first stop is Kelly Ingram Park. Ingram Park is sacred ground in the United States. It is here that the foot soldiers of the movement for freedom gathered to sing and organize and to begin and end their demonstrations. The blood of young and old watered this soil, now a lush park in a struggling part of the city. The Birmingham police brutalized their victims in this space by aiming water cannons at children, ripping the skin from their bodies, or by turning dogs loose on marchers who dared to turn a mirror on the brutality of white society.

Children joined the resistance also. They were met with brutality as well. In May 1963, thousands of them left school for the "Children's Crusades." They gathered at Ingram Park and participated in demonstrations for freedom. Eight hundred were carried to jail one day, filling up the available Birmingham jail space. Undaunted, more showed up the next day. Another six hundred were arrested for putting Jim Crow on trial at 16th Street North.

My first visit to Ingram Park took place a dozen years prior. While in town for another purpose, I made a pilgrimage to be in that space so sacred to the story of the struggle for freedom in the United States. I was young, still a seminary student, and clueless. I was also insatiably curious, so I was thrilled to walk upon a large public celebration. Luckily for me, this day was the celebration of the fortieth anniversary of the Children's Crusades. A ceremony for those children, now in their mid-fifties, was just ending. Four decades later, many of those "foot soldiers" carted off to jail in May 1963 had returned to Ingram Park to remember and to celebrate. And as I walked up, they were in small groups talking, reminiscing, and saying their goodbyes.

I sat down on a short wall and began a conversation with one man. He looked about the right age, so I guessed that he was there then, and was being celebrated on that day. I hoped he would be willing to talk. Sure enough, he was quick to explain the significance of the day to me. I listened eagerly.

Paul was his name. He wanted me to know that he was sitting on his bed getting dressed for church on September 15, 1963, when he felt the ground tremble. He knew immediately that something awful was happening. By the time he made it outside, there was mayhem in the streets.

We both looked to the handsome, Romanesque sanctuary across from the park as he gestured to it. "That's the place it happened," he said. "Not far from where that door is. The bomb blew a hole in the side of the building and killed those four girls. They were younger than me, but I knew their families."

He paused. Forty years later, we still needed silence to digest it.

He continued, "This is how it was: You see over there, on 15th Street?" He gestured now to the opposite corner. "In that storefront was a TV repair shop. And this is what life was like. Say I went in the TV repair shop to get a part for my TV. After waiting in line for three or four minutes, or even ten or fifteen, hell, maybe even an hour, it's my turn. But then, just before I ask my question, you come in. Now I have to move to the back and wait for you before I can get any service."

My insides roiled, and I silently lept to my own defense. *Now you wait a second, Mr. Paul. What do you mean "You"? You don't know that I've been reading books by Dr. King and that I used to live in a Black neighborhood and that I'm a loving Christian and I wouldn't have just stood there.* But I did not argue. His nonchalance convinced me that there aren't enough pages in Dr. King's books to make me any less white, or any less certain to have just stood there, silent and guilty. His "you" had no malice or anger or desire to wound. There was no yelling, nor any agitation in his voice. He just told me what, to him, was an unremarkable truth.

Paul's truth left me marked, like Jacob blessed with a limp as he comes back across the Jabbok River after his all-night wrestling match with a stranger.[4] Returning to Ingram Park, now with a group of young people on a ride toward freedom, I can still find that wall where Paul turned me around, where for the first time I could see that though we sat with our elbows bumping, the distance between us was miles apart. On this day, I dance between feeling that same distance, as I observe Alicia and Maria encounter the statue of a dog lunging at a foot soldier, and the feeling that we are not quite so far from one another now, that we have reduced the distance.

After we take some time in Ingram Park, our group walks across the street to Birmingham Civil Rights Institute (BCRI). The Institute includes a museum full of documentation and artifacts from the struggle for freedom from racism. A portion of the Greyhound blown up in Anniston is there. So is a pair of water fountains with "white" and "colored" signage above them. The experience puts visitors right there in the place where it happened when it first happened. BCRI reminds visitors in visceral ways that the history it presents is still alive. The Movement is not ancient history, but was within the lifetimes of many people alive today, people known to our group as parents and grandparents.

The museum, and the park, and the church have a physical effect. Each deepening revelation is a series of punches to the gut. The feeling is intensified by the realization that The Movement is being born again today. Around one corner is video of throngs gathering in the park with songs and chants and nothing to lose but their chains. Around the next is Bull Connor's armored tank made to meet non-violence with brutality. Around the next corner of the conscious mind is the unavoidable fact that the same scenes are being repeated in the streets of Ferguson and Baltimore, Charlotte and Cleveland.

Out in the streets of Birmingham, you can stand at the intersection of 6th Avenue and 16th Street North and observe in every direction the historical damage done by a society infected with racism. On three corners are BCRI, Ingram Park, and 16th Street Baptist Church. On the fourth is the shell of a one-story building. Behind that building is block after block of razed and destroyed city. This is where Paul lived, the man who told me

---

4. Genesis 32:22–32.

about my whiteness. His old house is gone now, as is every other house, for several blocks north. Stretching as far as you can see to the east and to the west, there is now an urban prairie of weeds and pavement. An interstate highway, mostly elevated above the ground, plows through around 20th Street, violently altering the landscape.

When planners and councils decided to build a superhighway through north Birmingham, they decided to leave Kelly Ingram Park, but to destroy the neighborhood around it. The life of the park was the people who occupied it. But those people were evicted from their homes and their blocks, their businesses and stoops. The place was better kept as a museum piece, the architecture says. This was public policy, done with public dollars and at the pleasure of those in power. The message of the interstate was clear to the neighbors it displaced—the struggle for justice had its epicenter here, and such a place cannot last.

Addie Mae Collins. Carole Denise McNair. Carole Robertson. Cynthia Wesley. Those four girls killed on the way to Sunday school had names and parents, siblings and schools, teachers and dreams and houses. They had mailboxes nailed to sides of houses in Birmingham, with little numbers to direct the postal carrier where to drop their birthday cards, houses probably in the sort of place that was destroyed to build highways not many years after their lives were taken. The girls could not be spared, nor could their neighborhood, because of the power of the great illusion that the distance between people cannot—or should not—be reduced.

So too do Tasha, and Crystal, and Imani—youth on the journey towards freedom—have names and parents and siblings, school and teachers and dreams and houses with mailboxes for birthday cards. Though there are alternatives, the powers and principalities keep building architecture that maintains the distance, that casts the foot soldiers as threats to law and order rather than as those who bring liberation for everyone. As we journey on, our imaginations keep drawing us closer together. We receive a word of inspiration from civil rights leader and community developer John Perkins in Jackson, Mississippi. We step with one another across the Edmund Pettus Bridge in Selma. We pull weeds and feed calves at Koinonia Farm in Americus, GA. And at every step, we do the simple, daily things that build the "Beloved Community" Charles spoke to us about—listening to one another, washing each other's dishes, singing our way down the highway.

⌁

John Coltrane was the grandson of a preacher. From his early days in small-town North Carolina, he heard the music of the church. Even as he became one of the most sophisticated improvising musicians the world has ever seen, his roots remained. The music of the church always returned. He was connected to his people, among other ways, through music.

Coltrane must have learned songs, in those early days after his birth in 1926, that had been passed down for generations. It is easy to imagine that the oldest members of his grandfather's congregation had been enslaved, had been emancipated, had lived through Reconstruction, and had witnessed the rise of Jim Crow. Through all of those historic moments, they would have kept adapting their songs, improvising new lyrics, adding new embellishments, and making sure the songs took roots in the hearts of the children around them. The cultural legacy of his people took root in John, becoming the building blocks for his world-shaking career.

Neither is it hard to imagine that John Coltrane as a child went to Sunday School more than a few times. He surely knew the energy of a Sunday morning. The play of children. The sound of the choir rehearsing before service. The laughter of menfolk telling stories from the week. The moans of grief and gratitude in the ladies' prayer circle. And, importantly, he would have known the safety of it all—the feeling of being in a physical and cultural sanctuary set apart from the cruelty of Jim Crow America.

Bombing a Sunday School is impossibly vicious. The bombing of 16th Street Baptist Church, and the permissiveness with which the white power structure in Alabama received it, became yet another example of the moral frailty of white society in the South. But across the nation, the increasing brutality with which white people were openly terrorizing Black communities, and the complete lack of accountability within white communities for their decrepit moral and legal positions, initiated changes. The bombing galvanized energy towards the passage of the Civil Rights Act of 1964. Law could not stop white terrorism of Black communities and people, but it could at least make it illegal. As a North Carolina native who had for years travelled the country making music, Trane knew what the fear of this sort of terrorism felt like. He felt a deep grief for his country and for his people. So, during a November 1963 recording date, only two months after the bombing, and four days prior to the assassination of John F. Kennedy, he introduced a new piece called "Alabama."[5]

"Alabama" stands in sharp contrast to almost all of Coltrane's other recorded work. Trane was a relentless innovator and a fearsome improviser. His playing was dense and complex, happening in rapid fire. At nearly impossible speeds, he explored ideas in every possible permutation and inversion. He was always searching, looking for new sounds and new ways of linking sounds and ideas together. Critics called his style "sheets of sound," because wave after wave of notes would inundate the listener. But "Alabama" is different. It is sparse, plaintive, and uncertain in a way that none of Trane's other recordings are.

The first note to sound is a drone that persists through most of the piece. Bassist Jimmy Garrison and pianist McCoy Tyner play a somber, brooding C minor chord that they will sustain through the entire first and last sections of the work. On top of this chordal drone, Trane enters with a plaintive melody. He is singing a song of lament. This is a new song, written in response to another new act in a history of cruelty, but the song comes from a specific place. It has been born from the tradition of field songs and blues. It has risen through jook joints and hush harbors, through Coltrane's bones and out of his lungs. Out of his soul.

The composition of the song reinforces a connection to the Elders. The melody is built from a single scale, called "pentatonic" because it has only five notes, rather than the seven notes common to most scales. The songs of the hymn choirs common in African-American tradition, the work songs of enslaved workers and chain gangs, and many of the marching songs common in the Civil Rights Movement are built from the pentatonic scale. It is the basic building block for folk music of all sorts, across many cultures. It lives deeply inside the bones and the souls of people for whom singing was one of few available survival strategies. Coltrane had learned a musical language he could turn to in moments of grief and trial. His people had passed down the knowledge of how to sing about violent, undeserved deaths. "Oh, sometimes it causes me to tremble," they sang. The existence of such songs testifies to how long they had suffered brutality visited upon their bodies and their communities, and to the ways they connected their story to the stories of other brutal deaths at the hands of cruel societies and emperors. In an interview, Coltrane spoke to this directly, stating that the Black musician does not need a

5. Coltrane, "Alabama."

justification for his art. . . It's built in us. The phrasing, the sound of the music attest to this fact. We are naturally endowed with it. You can believe all of us would have perished long ago if this were not so. . . You see, it is really easy for us to create. We are born with this feeling that just comes out no matter what conditions exist. Otherwise, how could our founding fathers have produced this music in the first place when they surely found themselves (as many of us do today) existing in hostile communities where there was everything to fear and damn few to trust? Any music which could grow and propagate itself as our music has, must have a hell of an affirmative belief inherent in it.[6]

Following the beginning section of "Alabama," featuring mostly sax, piano, and bass, the band moves into a more typical jazz setting. They take up a steady tempo. They "swing," to use the language common to the music. The tempo is gentle. The swing is light. But something more normal has returned. The drums join in for the first time, coloring the track and pushing it forward with work on the cymbals. But this brief move into a more normal formula does not last long. The track sounds like it falls apart after less than a minute, with Trane dropping out first, and the rest of the musicians coming to an abrupt halt shortly after. It falls apart in such a way that it sounds like a series of mistakes on the first few listenings. The musical landscape is ruptured.

And then, it happens. The drone returns. The melody sings the lament again. And now, Elvin Jones joins the lament on the drums. He plays with mallets, striking the toms with increasing weight and intensity. The sound is not unlike an explosion heard in the distance, like what Paul from Birmingham might have felt rumbling up through the foundations of his city on that September morning. The plaintive cry keeps sounding, and the rumbling refuses to cease.

The critic Amiri Baraka, writing in the liner notes to the album on which "Alabama" was released, said, "I didn't realize until now what a beautiful word Alabama is. That is one function of art, to reveal beauty, common or uncommon, uncommonly."[7] Coltrane reveals both lament and beauty in a new, yet traditioned, way. He writes a beautiful lament, titles it with a beautiful word, and sets it within a context that gives this particular event universal echoes. He draws from the long tradition that the elders of his

---

6. Hester, "Melodic Development of Coltrane's Composition," xxiii–xxiv.

7. Baraka, *Coltrane Live at Birdland*.

community knew and passed down, one they found echoed in the Psalms. Those elders and the psalmists knew that beauty often possesses people in a minor mode. It rises up from suffering that cannot be explained. Places that people grow to love with intensity and passion are also the places of deepest grief and aching. Even the most beautifully named places are comprised of gardens of suffering and hills that we might come to know as "the place of the skull."[8] Every geography has at one time been watered with tears, and more than once. To be connected to a place, and the people who inhabit it, is to join in the shedding of those tears. It is to sing songs, to build markers of memory that can wrestle beauty out of despair and create spaces of patient grief while grappling with a long, dark night.

⊷

This is how it happened, when it happened—two kids played an old trick. Both told their guardians they were going to the other's house for the night, and then they went for a late night walk. The thrill of exploring the neighborhood under cover of darkness, without supervision, is an old excitement. Everyone knows it. But something went wrong. One of them was carrying a gun, for a reason no one knows. And at the corner of Parkway and Tuckaseegee, some switch flipped, and one friend turned on the other. He fired two shots at close range, then flagged down a car to help and walked away.

2 a.m. Phone rings. "Look outside." Intersection taped off. Crime scene. Forty cops, detectives, investigators on the corner. They stretch down the street from the church next door to the bus stop in my front yard. Media hover at the edges.

I walk outside to inquire. Official silence. "Watch the news," they say. "You'll see this one."

I toss and turn for the next few hours. I know this scene, from other blocks, on other corners, near someone else's house. Somebody is dead. I do not want to know what comes next.

The block is quiet at 7 a.m. Nothing is on the news yet, but I know the streets will know. Sure enough, two young men are soon on the corner, standing and talking, shaking their heads at the dirt. I approach gently.

8. Matthew 27:23.

"Hey guys, do y'all know what happened last night?"
"Man, they took my brother, man. They took Khalil."

In the next moments I move through a heavy fog. Thick, molasses fog. It does not descend, but bubbles up through the ground, the ground where only a couple of hours ago Khalil was breathing his last breaths. The fog lodges first in my legs, which don't want to move. It keeps rising into my gut. I have never wanted so badly to throw up. My heart flutters in a way that would worry me, if I could worry. This is what it feels like when body and mind stop working together. My gut, my feet, my heart know something that cannot be uttered. My mind stammers, tries to form words, but they get lost on the way to my tongue. The misfiring of my heart and the trembling of my hands are the only language I have.

I stumble around, wishing for somewhere to go. And then it all comes into crushing reality when my four year old asks what is wrong with me. And Jesus Christ how do you explain the murder of his friend to a four year old? And then the phone starts ringing because it must have hit the news. And how am I going to tell Helms who does not know yet? And God damn it, Khalil is gone.

Sometime that morning, while the news is still making its way through the streets, a procession files down Tuckaseegee. I watch from the porch as it stops at the corner, on the soil made sacred overnight. Without any prompting, a circle forms. And there begins a great wailing. At the center is Khalil's mom, inconsolable. She is Rachel, weeping for her baby, because he is no more. Her brothers and sisters and her other children hold her as her body melts into the ground there. Moans too deep for words escape, over and over, bottomless, from every cell within her. There, where her youngest baby had lain, she waters the ground with her tears.

The chorus all weeps with her. A community of grief holds the corner, heedless of traffic, and stops the world for as long as they need to grieve. The procession of family and friends knows already what to do, and how to do it. They had gathered at home and walked to the place where it happened. They now hold space for those who need to weep to do so openly, without fear and in safety. In this moment, they have a language, a liturgy to draw from for how to be in the world when overcome with sorrow. Within it is the freedom to express everything that can be expressed. What can be expressed is insufficient—there are no words big enough to hold this grief.

This sacred moment, offered in full public view, is creating a space where the circle of those mourning can grow. What is most intensely personal to Khalil's mother and brothers is at the same time drawing others into a deep communal lament. The public expression of this grief moves it into the world, where it can be held and shared.

The pain is overwhelming. At the center of it, Khalil's mom is swept away in a roiling tidal wave of grief. There is no way to know which way to go for air. She weeps until she is weary with her moaning, until she is drowning in her tears.[9]

And yet, those present with her, full of grief themselves, know what to do. They know how to hold the family up, and how to hold one another up. They do that quite literally, and they know that when the next wave of tears hits them, they will be held up in the same way. This active knowledge, which appears intuitive, even instinctive, speaks of a deep resilience.

Such resilience, though, does not just spring up *ex nihilo*, out of nothing. It comes from somewhere, from a history, from cultural wisdom learned in living of history. The knowledge of what to do when a person is violently taken away exists because of the deep injustice rooted here. The injustice is built into the neighborhood in the same way the street pattern is. It is as obvious as the power lines stretched above each block, and at the same time as hidden as the underground lines that deliver and remove water from our houses.

Khalil's family and supporters appear to have some intuitive or in-stinctive insight into what to do in the hours following his death, but such insight is not purely innate. Grief is a natural human response, but they are demonstrating more than grief. They are observing a liturgy that has been learned to help families grieve deeply and well. Liturgies are developed over time and with practice. This family knows what to do because they have seen others do it. They have participated with others doing it. They may have done it themselves for other cousins or siblings, uncles or aunts. This is not the first time that violence has stolen away a beloved one on this corner, or in their lives.

In Enderly Park, as in other neighborhoods facing similar battles, this is the painful truth of life. The disease of violence, with all of its causes and all of its symptoms, lives here. Not only here, for sure. It pervades the whole society. It has visited our block today, and not for the first time. But faced

---

9. Psalm 6:6.

with violence, creative and ancient ways of grieving help people express, in hopes that later they can heal.

And yet, the conditions that create the need to grieve so many lives lost early persist. Violence still infects this land. No matter where or in what era, the people who experience the bloodiest, most vicious parts of our violent world are poor people and people of color. While the privileged remain relatively—though never completely—safe, Enderly Park holds vigils with some regularity. Sometimes for a child. The precise circumstances that lead to such a death are always different—the violence happens sometimes at the hands of someone whose back is similarly against the wall, and at other times because of violent policies enacted by men in alabaster buildings who are never close enough to see such grief. The ongoing existence of such violence, and especially the ongoing policy violence that builds conditions for street-level violence, are an expression of a society's collective will. The culture that cares about the death of Black children in impoverished, powerless neighborhoods does something about that powerlessness.

There is no easy or singular means of addressing the violent nature of American culture. We, and here I mean we white Americans, build much of our lives on the careful neglect of the traumatic reality our neighbors live with every day. James Baldwin once wrote, "Not everything that is faced can be changed. But nothing can be changed until it is faced."[10] The powers and principalities of our culture keep abdicating responsibility for the way that we place people of color in positions of precarity from birth. We ignore, we pretend, we refuse to see, and so we continue to re-enact the violent deaths of Black children. We could respond by pre-emptively attacking the conditions that lead to this grief being replayed over and over. But without fail, the fault always lies elsewhere, with someone else. We seem not to be able to share in the tears or to sit with those whose bones are shaking with terror.[11] This is a soul-shaking failure of imagination. It is a lack of love.

And yet, in the midst of such a culture, my neighbors have created ways to keep going. One way they have learned to keep going is by the intensely personal, but at the same time public, expression of grief that is happening on the corner on the morning of Khalil's death. This expression is part of what draws others in. And for the rest of the day, everyone is drawn in. It seems that almost everyone who ever loved Khalil gathered on the corner. Friends, cousins, church members, neighbors, teachers, principals, and bus

10. Baldwin, "As Much Truth As One Can Bear," 42.

11. Psalm 6:2.

drivers all show up. Hundreds of people come through. Many leave flowers in the spot where he died, or teddy bears, or balloons. The plastic pickets outlining the church yard become parchment for dozens of goodbye notes.

Rest in Peace, they say.

Rest in Power.

I love you.

Khalil died on the sidewalk, leaning against a broken plastic picket fence around the yard of a shuttered church building. While a real life passion play is going on in their yard, the church members are engaged in months of discussions about what to do with a building they no longer care about on a corner they no longer care about, in a neighborhood they can no longer be bothered with. Not one of their clergy shows up to grieve with the people or to offer a word of peace. Nor do they show up to repent of their neglect for the people and places that comprise the area they choose to own but not to occupy. That preaches, but not the message that Jesus wants the world to hear. To love our neighbor in the same way Jesus does requires our bodies. Our presence. It requires reducing the distance so that love and imagination can grow.

From the first moment I walked to the corner and learned what happened, I saw the blood smeared on the white pickets and across the sidewalk. During the initial grief of that morning, it becomes a visual connection to Khalil's broken body at a time when everyone is grasping for anything that will keep a connection. But after a short time, some family and friends begin to feel with great urgency that it is time to wash that stain away. Their guts are telling them that they can no longer see it, that they must hold to a picture of him full of life rather than to see the evidence of his body broken. Help clean it up, they plead. Someone clean it up.

Silently, Helms fills a bucket with water and brings a scrub brush. A wide path clears to sanctify the ground around her as she performs this sacred rite. She kneels, her chest heaving as she sobs. She begins to wash away the stain on the sidewalk. She cleans the fence. And having wiped it all down, she sends the water from the bucket streaming down the street. It flows past us, headed down to the bottom of the hill, where Stewart Creek will carry it into the Catawba River, which will carry it into the mysteries of the ocean.

Of Jesus's passion, the hymnwriter observes, "See from his head, his hands, his feet, sorrow and love flow mingled down." So too, at this passion, on this hill, do sorrow and love flow down, into the depths of the fathomless sea.

❧

There is a coda to "Alabama." It is one last attempt to resolve the lament. It builds quickly, growing louder and more intense in just a few short phrases. The tension mounts. The search for resolution grows. Then Trane makes the leap, on the penultimate chord. He lands high above the band, and attempts to change the mode from minor to major. He makes the musical equivalent of moving from grief to joy, from night to day. "Joy comes in the morning," the psalmist promises. But the move falls empty. Underneath the wailing saxophone, the harmony is cacophony, a series of overlapping dissonances. That note won't fit. The last try to move from weeping that has endured for many nights to a long-awaited joy only furthers the dissonance. And so the last chord returns home to its dwelling in deep lament. It rolls down in a flurry and settles low in a valley. There is nowhere else to go. There is no other chord to sound.

5

Jam Session[1]

THE NO. 1 TRAIN stops at Christopher Street. The doors slide apart, and dozens of riders file out and upstairs onto Seventh Avenue South. Walking northward toward Perry Street is an immersion in the sensory feast of Greenwich Village. This part of the city never stops. Cafes, clubs, shops, restaurants, offices, parks, traffic, and throngs of people all compete for any inch of space available. Quaint old-world housing sits next to glass and steel mid-rises. Trains rumble underneath. There is a man delivering pizzas by bicycle. A high-powered attorney wearing her business suit. A hipster who just spent half an hour trying to look disheveled. Students and shop owners walk by one way, artists and executives the other. There is enough energy packed into one hour in this Manhattan neighborhood to power the city of Charlotte for a week.

A walk to Perry Street is only four blocks. The whole world passes by on the way. Just north of Perry is the center of the world. A red awning stretches across the wide sidewalk. Small lettering announces the Village Vanguard. The Vanguard is to jazz as Cooperstown is to baseball, or the Louvre is to art. A visit is not an evening in a nightclub. It is a pilgrimage. A trip to the Village Vanguard is a descent into an underground cavern where

---

1. Rollins, "Tenor Madness." A "jam session" is usually an impromptu gathering where musicians can improvise together. They are mostly not recorded, but this track was recorded on a night when two legends—Sonny Rollins and John Coltrane—happened to be working in the same studio. The resultant impromptu session is one of the standard recordings of the music. It is the only known recording of Rollins and John Coltrane playing together.

Trane, Bird, Dizzy, Miles, Monk, and a whole roster of musical saints once transported listeners into other realms.

The line queues northward up the sidewalk. People seep slowly down into a dark womb where creation keeps happening. At the entrance, the doorman checks reservations, and then the walk down a creaking set of stairs begins. Giants have walked these steps. The mystery of being swallowed up into the same room those saints occupied begins to work the imagination. The anticipation builds until, seeping down, listeners finally enter into a plain, unimpressive space. Everything is painted in dark colors. Relics left by now-departed saints adorn the walls—album covers, photographs, signed promotional posters. People squeeze into chairs crowded around narrow tables. Pilgrims fill every possible space, ears open and hearts soften to what may happen this evening.

The evening liturgy begins with a brief warning on the public address system: turn off your phones; no recording; do not talk during the performance; don't forget to tip your server. Then, onto the stage walk some really average looking people. They are not the kind of characters anyone noticed on the subway on the way here, though they may have been on it. This is not the aesthetic of arena rock. There is little production, no fireworks or smoke machines. That is not what matters here. What matters becomes clear as creative, beautiful music begins.

Everyone remains silent. It is the kind of expectant silence that welcomes beauty into the world. Listeners eavesdrop in on the conversation taking place on stage, hearing the intimacy of someone's mind brought to expression by the rustling of air. The drummer accents the upbeat just right, spurring a melodic invention from the pianist. The bass lays down the foundation, providing a steady pulse and the harmonic bedrock to keep the conversation moving. The horn player listens in, adding flair with improvisation, drifting in and out of the guidelines with fleet fingers and fecund imagination. Most any night of the year, some of the best music in the world happens right in this little triangular room. Occasionally, something transcendent is born.

After taking in a set at the Vanguard, there are other options nearby to hear more music. Not far back down Seventh Avenue South is Small's. Again, listeners descend a long set of steps, give an offering to the doorman, and head into a small room. This room is packed, as it will be until 3 a.m. There is no table service, just rows of benches and chairs crammed in and oriented to a small bandstand. Lucky patrons might find two seats together at the bar where they can slide in, place an order, and turn towards the band to hear what will unfold.

On the bandstand are a cluster of musicians talking for a moment. Then, without speaking to the audience, someone snaps their fingers in time and says, "one . . . two . . . one, two, three, four." And they take off. The tune is Charlie Parker's "Thriving from a Riff." They play impossibly fast, and each person is featured for a short amount of time. There is no music written down, but everybody seems to know what to do, and they all support one another in doing it. The bass player drives everyone forward, the drummer throws his energy into the sizzle of the cymbals, and the horn players shout encouragement to their peers as the intensity picks up.

When the song is over, the horns go back in their cases. The pianist stands up and makes room for someone else. A different drummer steps up to the set and takes a seat. A trumpet and a trombone hop up to the front of the stand. Everyone shakes hands and introduces themselves. They don't know each other until now. Unless they have some secret knowledge, the chances seem slim that what follows will be worth listening to. How could they make anything beautiful without rehearsing and talking to each other? And yet, when the first lines of Dizzy Gillespie's "A Night in Tunisia" begin, they are all in sync. They thrill the whole room with the driving bass line, the complex drumming, and the screaming heights of the trumpet solo.

What happens in those moments appears to be musical alchemy. People who have never seen one another before come together around a stage. They quickly agree on a composition, exchanging only minimal words, and then begin playing. There is only the slightest organization visible, yet what unfolds over the following ten minutes is thrilling. And when it is done, more musicians shuffle in. They name another song, and the same process begins again. Players become listeners. Listeners turn out to be players. In short order, the whole room appears to be involved. Rapport builds among strangers, who risk new creations together. When the bartender issues the last call, people glance at their watches and see that morning comes racing. They have been lost in a world that nurtures underground creation, all of it built on a few riffs.

The jam session is an important way for musicians to learn, test material, and make connections with other musicians. Though it is informal, what happens is not a free-for-all, where anyone brave enough can show up and take a turn. The jam session has rules, which are unwritten, but well-known. They are learned by the instruction of elders within the tradition. The rules are caught by observation and practice, and they create an environment of supportive learning and experimentation.

Players who attend one of these sessions have to be a little brave. Working out new ideas requires lots of failure before sustained success comes. Hundreds, even thousands, of repetitions are required before a player can execute a new thought on an instrument. Getting it right takes a long time. Some ugly sounds will come out on the way to mastery.

Listeners must also be brave because sometimes the people doing the experimenting aren't very good. Everyone comes at their own level. But every participant, even the most seasoned professional, remembers their own failures in just this setting. Such memory works against a session becoming a competition. The objective is not to outdo anyone, but instead to participate in the creation of something beautiful. Everyone can have a role in building that beauty.

The same conditions that lead to the magic of musicians who do not know each other coming together to create beautiful music occur around the supper table, at a book club, or anywhere people gather to interact. In most of those places, it is unnecessary to post rules or regulations. People who gather for supper together regulate themselves without the need for writing down guidelines. Friends reading together in a book club do not need formal governance. Pick-up basketball governs itself by the participation of players and the rules of the court. At some point though, someone will show up who either does not know the rules or chooses not to abide by them. The person who breaks the boundaries tests the strength of the community. Does the gathered group have the resilience to correct the offender, but at the same time the grace to draw him in? Is there enough conviction about the value of the gathering to confront the person who threatens it?

It only takes one offender to destroy the hard work a community has done to establish a sense of mutuality and care for the other. If a musician comes to the jam session and inserts a spirit of competition into the evening, the others gathered are confronted with the challenge of drawing him into beauty without alienating or marginalizing. Perhaps an elder of the community can offer a word of reproof. Maybe a friend will pull the offender aside and remind him of the rules. If the offender is not drawn into the way the community works, though, it can alienate everyone present. The fun ends for the listeners and the players. People will leave and will stop returning.

Moments of challenge to a community are risky. Strong groups develop the resilience to withstand difficulties. Some can meet challenges and at the same time bring an outsider into the communion that is already happening. Weak groups may fall apart when such a test appears, or may choose to keep both conflicts and outsiders away because they lack the strength to incorporate them. Confrontation takes courage. It requires valuing the present community enough that the risk is worth it.

⟠

The main thoroughfare of Enderly Park is Tuckaseegee Road. Tuck, as neighbors call it, stays busy throughout the day. My street intersects Tuck just a few feet from my house. The presence of a church, a government building, and multiple types of housing at this intersection marks its historic importance as a neighborhood center. Tuckaseegee is an important thoroughfare for people coming and going around downtown. Our street, Parkway Avenue, is of historical importance because it was the way to the old amusement park that used to sit at the bottom of the hill. People would rush along Tuckaseegee for work Monday through Friday, and then on Saturday and Sunday stroll down Parkway Avenue to Lakewood Park to ride the boats, or the ferris wheel, or to have a picnic. Today the amusement park is gone. Now Parkway makes important connections to industry, to other neighborhoods, and to a bus line that gets crowded during rush hours. The intersection is important to many people, which is obvious by the lines of traffic that back up during morning and evening commuting periods.

As I am writing today, the power is out on my block, including at the intersection just a few yards from me. The stoplight that governs the intersection is not working, which is concerning. Given the relentless pace of a city, with everybody always in a hurry to get to wherever is next, I am concerned about the increased potential for a collision. I am feeling this concern in my body. My ears are attuned to any sounds that may indicate an accident has happened. My legs are a little jumpy, as though they are ready to run and help if needed. I know the awful sound of a car crash, and my gut is preparing to roll into a knot at the first hint of that terrible sound.

Often in a power outage, a police officer shows up to direct traffic in the absence of a functioning signal. Today no officer arrives. But for the hour that the light remains out, I am observing a most remarkable thing—there are no collisions. People are regulating themselves. They all slow down, alarmed by the signal that is not working. They are concerned for their own safety and for what other drivers may do. Pedestrians are crossing without issue. Everyone is getting where they need to be. Bikers, box trucks, cars, pedestrians, buses, and 18-wheelers are all negotiating the intersection in a neighborly fashion.

Not only is the intersection working in absence of the direct oversight of the signal, it is actually working more efficiently than usual. Because of the timing of the signal facing Parkway Avenue, there is almost always a line of traffic idling near our house. The green is too short and the red too long. The lengthy red is an irritant for drivers. It encourages speeding when there is even a slight chance to squeeze through a yellow. I start almost every car trip by sitting impatiently waiting for the light to change, or by hopelessly peeling out of the driveway to try and catch the tail end of the green light. Which never works, but that does not stop me from trying.

The traffic condition is not a good situation for neighborhood children, who breathe the air near the stoplight. Too many trucks and buses idling for lengthy periods means a steady dose of exhaust for the many kids moving up and down Parkway and Tuckaseegee in the afternoons. This is one of the reasons that asthma is far more common in poor urban neighborhoods like ours than wealthier ones. Idle traffic fouls the air and fouls children's lungs. Little things like stoplight timing and truck traffic have long-term cumulative effects on the health of places and people.

But on this day without a stoplight, no one sits idling. Cars pull up to the intersection, wait for a safe moment to pull through, and continue on their way. There is no line of traffic. There are no big rigs waiting on a long light cycle while puffing diesel exhaust into our air. Our place is a little more pleasant for this hour, a little quieter, a little less frantic.

I worry about the power outage because I have learned to see my safety and my neighbors' as being assured by the presence of an outside authority who can negotiate the ways our lives intersect with one another. Going through thousands of stoplights has taught me to think of intersections in one particular way. Without a functioning signal to intercede, my mind assumes danger. I have been trained to think that without the assistance of an expert—in this case, a traffic engineer—my life and the lives of my neighbors are in danger. I assume that without an intervention, people would not naturally seek the safety of themselves and others.

But at least on this day, that is not the case. Neighbors are acting neighborly. Even when someone ignores the signs of potential danger and speeds right through the intersection, everyone else is looking out for danger, which protects themselves, but also protects other people. The neighbors are taking care of the scofflaws, even if the scofflaws do not realize it. Because nearly everyone is aware of the need to regulate themselves, those who are negligent, either with or without intention, also find a safe place within the community. Resilient communities hold themselves together even when put under the stress of danger.

One hour of a power outage at a moderately busy intersection during the middle of the day does not disprove the need for traffic signals. Stoplights have their place. But going without this one for a little while is a glimpse into the possibility that all communities have. The signs given to create meaning and to bring order to societies—in this case, the stoplight being a symbol of order and safety—may say more about the people who created the sign or signal than about those who use the sign every day. In other words, that someone in an official capacity determined the need for a signal and a set of laws around it to govern the potential conflicts arising at the intersection of two streets does not mean that is what is actually needed. It may be that communities already have the resources and people needed to negotiate simple intersections, and even complex ones, without destroying one another.

The kind of eyes we bring to any situation determine what we see there. If at every crossroads we expect a functioning stoplight and full compliance from all drivers about the laws governing that stoplight, then any situation that does not meet those expectations will look like danger. Looking for the symbols we have been trained to think of as signs of safety—e.g., traffic signals—but not seeing them makes it easy to miss the actual process of community life happening in plain view.

Learning to see by focusing on what is missing, like a stoplight during a power outage, is the essential idea behind the "Broken Windows" theory of policing. The basic image of this theory is that an empty building with one unrepaired broken window is far more likely to develop more broken windows than a building with no broken windows. Once many broken windows appear, other problems in the structure are sure to follow. In short, problems tend to aggregate together. One small symptom of a loss of vitality—the broken window—is a strong indicator of more problems to come.

Applied to policing, law enforcement departments seek to identify the areas of town where there are "broken windows," both literally and figuratively. In those areas, they look for particular types of small problems clustered together—public drunkenness, loitering, excessive noise violations, infrastructure decay, decrepit housing, and so on. Those areas become the targets of aggressive policing of small violations. Citizens may be ticketed and even arrested for any sign of potentially illicit activity. The theory behind this strategy of policing is that by aggressively targeting the small signs of broken communities, more traumatic crime—assaults, homicides, gang activity—can be stopped before it starts. My grandfather might have called this the Barney Fife approach—"We've got to nip it in the bud!"

There are multiple problems with Broken Windows Theory policing. One is that it assumes there is only one type of problem—willful infractions of public order by individual actors. This assumption works on the idealistic and simplistic notion that there are two, and only two, elements at play. One is the law, which is assumed to be just, and the other is the citizen or neighbor. In the area where the "broken windows" strategy is deployed, residents are assumed to be always close to breaking the law. In the "broken windows" part of town, everyone is a criminal.

In Broken Windows policing, the most-used tactic is to stop violations of the law before they happen through many minor interactions. "Stop and frisk" strategies derive from the Broken Windows theory. Interactions with police do not require reasonable suspicion. The more stops, the better. Poor people, and especially poor people of color, bear the brunt of this strategy through many needless interactions with agents of the state over the course of a lifetime.

Using the analogy of a vacant building, the tacit assumption made in the Broken Windows Theory is that broken windows are always caused by vandals throwing rocks. This is not true. When buildings develop foundation issues, one symptom that can indicate a problem with the foundation is cracked glass. If the structure that a building rests on is unstable, that may first become visible in broken glass, which is unable to absorb the shifting pressures of a faulty building. Broken windows may appear well before cracks in brick foundations become visible.

On the level of neighborhoods, Broken Windows thinking functions on the idea that signs of distress will beget more, and worse, signs of distress. The way to combat further issues with crime in a distressed place, then, is to fix those troubling symptoms quickly. But there are other questions that may help to understand distressed spaces better. It could be that the foundation upon which a building rests is flawed, perhaps fatally so.

Who built the building? For whom did they build it? Were the builders part owners also, ensuring more careful work? What was the quality of the materials used? How long was it intended to last? Has regular maintenance been done to address issues as they appear?

The quick fix of replacing a broken window pane hides the terrifying revelation that might be discovered by examining the base of the structure. Foundation issues are the worst news a building owner can get. Snooping around the foundation of the structures that keep places like Enderly Park poor and powerless is likely to reveal centuries of structural issues that have never been addressed. The names for some of those foundational issues are redlining, urban renewal, Jim Crow, mass incarceration, and chattel slavery.

It is hard to get the news that your building's foundation is cracked. It is harder still to make the necessary repairs to fix it, or perhaps even to tear it down and build a new, firmer foundation. It is far easier to fix a broken window pane, but if you do that, you'll always be fixing broken window panes.

When an officer trained in Broken Windows policing enters into a poor community, his training has taught him to see all of the potential for crisis that is happening. He has discretion to actively pursue the elimination of those potential crises. Every person is a potential threat rather than a potential gift to the community. Broken Windows policing is not unlike the way that many people see poor communities. Missionaries, social workers, commuters, and even residents of those neighborhoods themselves can be susceptible to Broken Windows thinking. This is like seeing a stoplight during a power outage and focusing on a danger that needs intervention, rather than observing the way community is happening on the ground. Both circumstances are happening in the same space. The eyes brought to a situation determine which circumstance is seen.

✻

One blessed memory along Tuck is our friend Skeet. He was short and thin, with sleepy-looking eyes that only half opened. Out of those eyes he saw far more than his share of trouble. Truth be told, he brought a fair portion of it on himself. His hard living was both the cause and the effect of his serious problem with alcohol. Skeet almost always had a buzz going, as he did one afternoon when he showed up on the porch.

"I'm ready to make a change," he said. His words were slurred together.

"You getting tired of this daily existence, running from one drink to another?" I asked.

"That's right. And I've got to do something different," he said.

"I'll help you get in the right place if you want," I said.

He hugged me. "I know you will, 'cause you love me," he said, and then he stumbled off the porch and headed back to the corner store. He assured me he would be back.

The next day when I caught up to him, he did not remember our conversation, and was no longer keen on making changes. So it was with Skeet.

I was never exactly sure where Skeet lived. It would not have been hard to find out, but there was no need. If I wanted to find him, there was one particular corner of Tuck where he was almost always available. It was, of course, an intersection within an easy walk of the corner store. There he sat, on a milk crate turned upside down—his outdoor living room, from which he wore a rut in the sidewalk on the way to the store.

Because he never had it all together, Skeet was vulnerable to being taken advantage of. Sometimes this might mean being roughed up by a neighborhood bully looking to take his pocket change. At other times it might mean being subject to encounters with the police, who saw him as a nuisance. This resulted in more than a few stints in the county jail, though Skeet was never a danger to anyone other than himself. Other folks often talked down to him, and saw him as the worthless character standing on the corner during the middle of the day while responsible adults have jobs. With that sort of vision, Skeet was the embodiment of all the problems plaguing Enderly Park. When you can only see broken windows, Skeet looks only like a broken man. But no person or neighborhood is only broken. And what is broken is often not what is most interesting.

What the folks closest to the ground knew was that Skeet helped hold Enderly Park together. The good thing about Skeet always being on the corner was that *Skeet was always on the corner*. He saw everything. If anything happened, Skeet witnessed it. If something went wrong at the corner store, he watched it go down. If someone was cutting school, he saw them and gave them an earful about it. When someone got arrested or went to the hospital, Skeet knew, and could help make sure a carload of neighbors went for a visit to the jail or the hospital. There was the problem of Skeet being able to communicate clearly who and what he had seen, but eventually you would figure it out if it was important enough.

The urbanist Jane Jacobs noted the importance of "eyes on the street" in the life of thriving urban neighborhoods. The more eyes around, she thought, the more safe and vibrant a neighborhood becomes. The presence of people creates safer conditions for other people. A walk down a city block humming with people feels far different than a walk down a block as the only person around. Isolated spaces leave people more vulnerable to abuse or harm because there is no one else to witness what is happening. The presence of even a few strangers can change the feeling of that same walk, enabling the walker to slow down and notice the birds singing, or the careful trim work on a house, or the neighbor who speaks from her porch.

Skeet had a crew of buddies he spent his days on the corner with. They were constant eyes on the street. From the outside, they looked like a well-known type—ne'er-do-wells who hang out on a stoop all day; lazy, refusing to work; beggars; likely to commit crime. From the inside, things look very different. The number of people on the corner at midday who work second- and third-shift jobs becomes plain. The deep value of the relationships forged on the corner is made obvious. The guys on the corner build solidarity among people living on the margins, creating a natural network of mutual aid and care in a place of need. And for folks like Skeet, being there becomes meaningful work that builds community. He knew that his presence in that place mattered, though no one was paying him or even thanking him. That's one of the reasons he kept showing up, day after day. This is how vibrant community works—people take responsibility for one another. They find ways to be of use to each other, and they build meaning and pleasure from that. And they include strangers, like me, into their networks of care and solidarity, until those strangers become friends.

Conversion, like with Paul, struck down on a street corner between Jerusalem and Damascus, is a way of naming the gift of new eyes. Getting converted is getting your vision set right, so that the wild goodness of God comes shining through, refracted and glimmering even through broken panes. Conversion makes things look different. What appears to be a burden turns out to be a gift. The brother who always looks like a problem is a brother who ought to be celebrated. And a pilgrim encountering everyday holiness becomes like Jacob at Bethel, who awakes from his slumber in the pink morning light of an ordinary Wednesday, and knows that "this place is holy, though I knew it not."

Khalil died in the first hours of a Tuesday morning. Khalil's family made their visit to the place where he died not long after dawn, and then retreated to a home a safe distance away to mourn together. As other neighbors get the news, they head to the corner where it happened. They come to sit on the ash heap. They refuse to be consoled. By mid-morning, the crowd swells to dozens of people just milling about, crying on one another's shoulders. It includes all of the youth and children with whom we shared our days during that summer. Teachers, principals, bus drivers, church members, all kinds of family, and an impossible number of friends come. People who did not know Khalil, but know someone who loved him, show up. There is nothing for anyone to do. Everyone arrives with the sense of needing to linger there.

For the rest of that day, we linger. We just stay there. There is nothing to do, yet no one can go home. Being there, on the corner, together, is the only thing anyone can think of to fit the moment. So that is what we do. While we sit, we talk about Khalil. We laugh at the way he would drive the older kids crazy with his constant play. Or how he would turn up the charm while flirting with girls several years older than him. We search for little relics—a picture, an item we recall him using. Someone brings his old bike and leans it against the fence. It stays there for months, untouched.

Losing a beloved does not settle in all at once. The enormity of a loss keeps sneaking up from behind. A memory brings a laugh, and the chance to work a little further into the new given. Each passing hour is a chance to enter one more step into its room, swiping blindly at the wall in hopes of switching on a light. Without warning, laughter changes back into tears, into sobs and heaves and groans. New and old worlds keep bumping against one another, and with great pain at first. With pain to rock the foundation.

Eyes adjust haltingly to the new room, sometimes closing rather than facing the bleak interior. There is no way back. The corridor behind the door is long and dark and the flooring has been ripped away. Only imagination can reach back to what was. No matter how deep the longing, no one returns to the old space. Both tears and laughter, gifts expressed from within bodies that ache and hurt, begin to shine dim light in this new room. Another step inside yields more light, but also more longing not to be here. It is still dark. The desire to be elsewhere still rules. And yet, there is nothing to do but to settle into this new space, to keep working into it while it works to get bone-deep, to envelope its occupants into an unwanted newness of life.

So a journey of grief may proceed for months or years, in wild and unpredictable ways. On this Tuesday, we are just beginning a wilderness wandering. We only know that for now, we will wander together. There is no way to grasp where this will take us. Youth, adults, friends, strangers—we stand at the corner. We sit on the church steps. We maintain this space that we cannot bear to think about, but cannot stand to leave.

As grief unfolds, friends show up with food. Khalil's family, in their own space, is overwhelmed with visitors and gifts. At the corner of Tuck and Parkway, our youth room also begins to fill with chicken and biscuits, with pies and cakes to nourish and comfort the young people keeping vigil. Preparing food is a way of acknowledging utter uselessness when faced with tragedy. "I know there is nothing I can do to make things better," the cook says, "but I have a great recipe for chicken casserole. And this fruit salad is a way of saying 'I love you.'"

No one is hungry for a long time, but we understand what the giver is saying. And maybe this is one of the best gifts. It is tender care that feeds the body weak with grief. It is care that can be left in silence, without disturbing. The giver offers a piece of herself through labor and time and care. The gift is a tangible reminder of the presence of a community of support.

This dog day afternoon in mid-August lingers. The sun makes its way down Tuckaseegee Road, setting at the far end of the street. Dusk takes the edge off the heat, but the summer air remains thick and sticky. Seeing the light waning reminds our bodies that we will somehow move to Wednesday. And the movement of the sun begins to stir within our young people a need to create for themselves and their neighbors an expression of their mourning. By suppertime, we are beginning to discuss a vigil to honor Khalil, hosted and directed by the youth of Enderly Park. The young people sense that today they need to sit, but tomorrow they will be ready, slowly, to act.

With the family's blessing, we begin planning on Wednesday morning for a vigil the following night. Jade will sing. Alicia and Danielle will speak. The children will release balloons. Comments from the community will be welcomed. I am to offer a word of peace to close the vigil. We will hold it in the only place possible—at the spot where Khalil breathed his last. On the grounds of the abandoned church next door.

The abandoned church. The building sits with stained glass covering its lack of life. The only life the modest brick building will have seen in years is a vigil for a murdered child. No potluck dinner on the grounds. No children playing tag while adults carry on committee meetings. No hymn tunes echoing into the streets. Where are their Christians? Where is their God? Did their Christ also drive a shiny car out to the suburbs to get a piece of the dream? Did he also want plenty of parking, a gym, different neighbors, better return on investment? The Christians, they worship a dead man come to life on Sunday morning, but cannot bear to be with the dying and broken-hearted during the week. This is a Broken Windows Theology—in America, the churches do things to the poor, but they cannot bear being with the poor.

The places with the broken windows get the bus ministry. The bus ministry is when the suburban church picks up the kids from a poor neighborhood on Sunday morning on a bus. The volunteers promise cookies and lemonade, plus a ride on the bus with the cool paint job. They drive off as heroes to save the children. Later the volunteers will tell harrowing tales about their dangerous bus journey across the railroad tracks. They are living out a bold faith, risking themselves in order to save those poor souls. In the neighborhood, the bus ministry is a weekly reminder that church people do not think your place is worth inhabiting.

In broken windows theology, churches, like police departments, wrongly identify what is happening in a place, and act on their assumptions to enforce a social structure that cannot liberate anyone. Christians, especially white Christians, see what they think are "broken windows" and try to help with little initiatives and projects that attempt to get at the visible distress without addressing the problematic foundations that concentrate the strain of society in certain places. Perhaps congregations address those outward signs with a "feeding ministry" or a clothing closet. On the appointed day, some poor people get fed a meal in a soup line. Others serve the meal in the soup line. Such works of mercy can serve an important role, but they also reinforce who has power and who does not. Rare is the ministry that bursts the boundaries of who serves and who gets served. Dinner tables are the perfect place for breaking boundaries, for nourishing the kind of community that can heal the brokenness of the world. But tables can also reinforce brokenness. Typically, some people leave with bellies full, and others do not sit down to eat, but leave feeling useful. Nobody gets free.

Or it may happen like this: the volunteer ministries spend hours each week working in the clothes closet. They receive donations, sort through clothes, do paperwork, open up, and then stay after to clean up. For one morning, as the result of several days worth of work, they give away leftover clothing to people who need meaningful work to do, and the opportunity to earn a wage from it. Everyone plays a pre-scripted part, the volunteers always controlling access to excess goods, the needy always filling out forms and being herded into lines. And at the end of the day, those who lack still do not have what they need. Those with too much still believe that more stuff is essential to the good life. Nobody gets free.

What Christians have come to think of as mission is mostly poverty tourism. It is a broken windows theology. Folks get close to some poor people for a little while—perhaps an hour, maybe a week—but almost never ask why poor people are poor, or how churches and church members profit from their poverty, or how to break those systems that bind everyone into haves and have-nots. To serve soup in an area with outward signs of decay takes a couple of hours per day. Jesus is not interested in a couple of hours. He wants lives. He demands souls. He will tear down temples and sanctuaries built on sand in order to rebuild them with the rejected stones of the world. Nothing less than rebuilding a church in ruins will be sufficient.

Rebuilding a church in ruins is part of what God is doing through the young people of Enderly Park as they plan the vigil for Khalil. They decide the steps of the empty church will form the altar. The planning continues, and we begin to spread the word. There is no formal announcement. There are no fliers. No need. Word moves quickly on Tuck. By the time the event arrives, hundreds are crushed together on a stifling August evening. The yard around the church is no match for the crowd. People spill into the streets. Traffic slows to a crawl, which does not matter because for those gathered the world has stopped. Dozens of mourners are across Tuckaseegee Road watching, partly because there is no more space, and partly in hopes that if they do not get too close it will not really be true. Local media all hover around. They are ready to pounce on the grieving family to get an interview for the nightly newscast.

At one point during the vigil, a little noise springs up in the crowd across the street. I can see a small disturbance going on, but it resolves quickly. Focus remains on the liturgy of grief unfolding on the church steps. Jade sings. She trembles at the edges of the notes. The power of her breath takes a moment to build from a wobble into a clear note. While her voice is weak with grief, the Spirit animates her with mysterious strength.

Danielle has a hard time getting through the words of her prayer. There are so many tears inside her yearning to come out. But the presence of the Christ hovers there with her over the chaos of her tears. She cries and speaks. She speaks, then cries. And the Spirit turns her prayer into a creative, healing force.

Other neighbors speak. The crowd offers shouts of support when a cousin begins a song that she cannot finish. They grow restless when a man with a trite speech and marketing materials for his nonprofit takes over the mic. Khalil's father, through the haze of his own trauma, speaks with beauty and power about compassion and the possibilities of forgiveness for the troubled young man who killed his son.

The children write messages and tie them to balloons. They release them, carrying unspeakable prayers in hopes they might be heard in the heavens. Those balloons—and our letting go of them—say everything our bodies can say about the deep grief of that day. Though words do not come easily, we all know the meaning of our eyes lifted up towards a beyond that we cannot see or know.

On the way up, the oak tree on the corner grabs some balloon-prayers. It holds them. It keeps them, red ribbons wrapped in its tangle of branches, from sailing away to wherever prayers go. It had been watching, that old oak. That old willow oak, planted on that corner when the neighborhood was built, was watching. That old sprawling willow oak, when it was still learning how to be a tree, watched piles of bricks being stacked into a sanctuary. It saw families headed for picnics at the amusement park. When the land speculators came through during white flight, using fear and racism to break up the neighborhood, the old oak watched. When new families came in, having had their homes in other places taken and their trees ripped up, the old willow oak was ready to offer shade for parents and leaves for kids to pile up and jump into. When Khalil exhaled his last breath under its canopy, that old oak breathed it in, watchful, still.

For all those years, that willow oak stayed, unmoved. It saw things beautiful and horrible, but never interfered. It only did its job. Dropping leaves. Nesting birds. Making shade. Until today. Arms outstretched, the tree snatches a prayer and wraps its long ribbon into a jumble. Why today? Why, after 80 some years of stillness, reach out now? Why not intercede on the day that it happened?

The tree ruins the poetry of the moment, the balloons all sailing away out of sight into the by-and-by. But maybe prayers belong in old willow oaks. Up high, but tied to the ground. Released but rooted. Not floating off into parts unknown. Here, present, with us. In the neighborhood.

We sing as the balloons soar with our prayers. I am singing, but not because I believe what I am singing. The old song is about the release of burdens and about God's abiding peace. I cannot believe in this, at least not on this day. I sing hoping to believe. Maybe soon, but not today. There is no blessed assurance that things will be alright in Enderly Park.

Tears and hugs abound. Those gathered do the only thing people can do, which is to hold one another up when no one would blame them for just falling down.

I learned later about the noise in the crowd across the street, the small commotion during the vigil. The energies of the evening spilled over into a little scuffle. Two guys bearing witness there, overflowing with righteous grief and anger, had their tempers flare. This hardly seems unusual. Packed tightly into a small space, and experiencing a trauma unlike anything Enderly Park had experienced in many years, if ever, a couple of guys got overheated. In testimony to the resilience of the gathered community, the potential for a large conflict was quickly resolved by another neighbor. Brother Keith gathered them in. A young man himself, just barely over twenty, he had the wisdom to offer them another way to express their rage. He helped create comfort by offering some extra space and a listening ear. He held his huge arm around one of the young men, and welcomed him into a safe place to let go of some grief.

In a most difficult time, Keith showed that Enderly Park was—and is—resilient enough to gather in those who threatened to break up the community. There was no need to call for outside help to care for those gathered. Neighbors were doing it themselves. We were doing it ourselves. Strong leaders like Keith helped make sure of that. In light of the violence that had gathered us, the scuffle and its quick resolution was a powerful demonstration of the strength of the community.

The crowds linger into the night. They continue to strengthen one another as long as they stay. The story that is being worked out on the corner is as deep as the roots of that oak tree. At a time of chaos, neighbors are doing exactly what neighbors do. They are loving one another. They are creating a space for healing and release. In a place where trauma has happened, beauty is reclaiming the street. You can see it in the tears and the hugs, in the laughter and the reunions of people who have not seen one another for years. The spirit of the place is being revived, slowly, and in recognition of the complexity of the space, where goodness and profound loss are mingling together in the same soil. The people are doing it themselves, led by the youth who called them together on this night to remember Khalil.

Later, as we settle in for the evening, Helms and I flip on the news to see the images of the vigil. Though we should not be surprised, we respond in horror to what we see. The late news leads with the scuffle.

"Troubled neighborhood spills over into violence again at vigil for peace," the anchor read.

All of the work. All of the tears. All of the energy and grief our youth spilled into this beautiful moment, and the first thing reported to the two million people in our region overlooks all that beauty. It would have been better to remain silent. Instead the story was the broadcast of one reporter's fear—fear built on unexamined racism—as though it were truth. The truth was not so sensational, but it was so much more beautiful.

The reporter saw what he was conditioned to see. The only eyes he possessed were trained to see trouble on our side of town, so that is what he saw. The viewers watching that evening were conditioned to see trouble in Enderly Park. That is what they saw. That is still what they see. The "inner city" is the place of perpetual crisis, of constant danger.

The reporter entered a new landscape with the same old eyes. He reported the same racist tropes that have helped maintain racial oppression for centuries. He saw savages, unable to control their passions.

Here is what you could see, with different eyes: you could see a peaceful gathering of people enduring an unexplainable trauma. You could see extraordinary, uncontainable energy given to speech and action. You could see a neighborhood with the resources to deal with difficulty. One evidence of this was that Keith intervened in the scuffle. He helped to console those whose emotions were raging, and to offer a step towards healing.

There were other things to see, things you might highlight in a report from the scene at Tuckaseegee and Parkway. Things like traffic slowing, even stopping, to honor the lives of those gathered and to honor the life taken there. You might see the worship of God as voices cried out laments and sang songs of peace, uttered words of solidarity and prayers of hope. You could certainly see courage and resilience in a most trying time. This community was operating by unspoken but deeply known rules about mutual care during a moment of crisis. By the force of love, people from many places were welcomed as participants in this act of improvisation towards healing.

The ground on which we stood the night of that vigil is holy ground. The blood of a beloved and the tears of many loved ones sanctified it. That holy ground holds stories that have as their primary characters creative people who have built a place of thriving in the midst of struggle and heartbreak. They have welcomed me into their story. The meaning and the best use of that ground began to come into question in the days that followed. In the midst of that struggle, and every other one, there stands an old willow oak tree, rooted in earth, reaching towards heaven.

6

Backwater Blues[1]

KHALIL WAS KILLED IN August 2012. In February 2013, only six months later, there is a knock at my door while I'm making Sunday lunch, right after church.

"Brother Greg, somebody shot Keith," Danielle says.

This cannot be true. I am not willing for this to be true. My insides are begging for this not to be true. My guts send out the groans that the Spirit can interpret when words will not come. While my spirit protests, my body moves. I run down the street to the chaotic scene, just one block west of the last crime scene.

Yellow tape cuts across Tuckaseegee Road. It flaps in the wind as it encircles the field, brown in winter, that stretches under the tall power poles. Mourners push up against the tape, reaching over, shouting questions. "Who was it? Who did this?" A helicopter circles, snooping in vain for a lead. An ambulance has already sped away in a hopeless attempt to revive Keith's brutalized body. The word is that he is dead, shot multiple times by someone who was seen running across the brown field, and who will never be identified in the years that follow. The crowds grow, but the grief is different this time. It feels exhausted, like there are no tears left in the reservoir.

My mind refuses the new reality. I insist to someone that before we all lose our composure, we need to be sure which Keith they are talking about. But we all know there is only one Keith in Enderly Park. He is kind, a trait he displays with his big, welcoming grin. Keith loves kids, and kids

1. Smith, "Backwater Blues."

86

love him, not least for his wrestling matches with them. Keith, with a knack for fishing and a quiet resilience that he has begun to harness for himself, his family, his baby on the way. That Keith is gone. I am trying to protect myself from something for which there is no protection. In desperation I am trying to protect other people from something our society has never been willing to protect them from. I know this, but my mind cannot hold the new knowledge yet. Finally, as the new reality settles in, I walk back to the house to inform the others in the community.

When I share what has happened, I am matter-of-fact about it, as though something ordinary has occurred. As though the world is not crumbling again for people we love, and for us as well. The feeling of numbness remains for a long time. The trauma is still too much, six months after Khalil. I cannot meet the intensity of the event this time. The violence has taken something from me. It has built a wall. I still do not know how long it takes to climb over this wall, or to tear it down.

As the new reality settles into me, my guts are screaming, "Leave! Get out of there!" Overwhelmed, still not healed, I cannot go through this again. At some point in the afternoon, I grab my children and get out of the neighborhood. We wind up in an indoor hotel pool courtesy of a friend. The kids squeal with delight in the water, but I can't return their joy. I just ache.

I never question whether I should continue living in Enderly Park. This place is home. These people are my people. I belong to them, and them to me. But the day of Keith's murder raises something new within me. For the afternoon, I do what many people have been expecting me and Helms to do for a long time—to take our kids and get out.

From the beginning, folks thought that's what we would eventually decide. "You guys are living there now," some said, "but what will you do when you have kids?"

"You'll have to move when you have children," others said. "Surely you do not want to send them to school over there."

"When are you going to get a real job, with benefits and all? And insurance for your kids?"

Moving out has never really occurred to me and Helms. With QC Family Tree, we are trying to create a space of "rooted discipleship in West Charlotte." When you have deep roots, you do not leave a place easily. But on the day of Keith's murder, the instinct to take my kids away, to protect them from the awful thing that has just happened, is strong. I am having a hard enough time dealing with the killing myself. I cannot imagine how, or even whether, to tell a two-year-old and a four-year-old that yet again, someone who delights in seeing them, and someone whom they delight in seeing, has been gunned down in the streets, at a place we can see from our front porch.

I am not afraid for their physical safety, nor am I afraid for my own. But I am terrified of how proximity to violence may affect them. I wonder when the trauma of knowing what happened will come back. Will it be in a year? In five years? Ten? There is no guarantee that it will return in a way that I will be able to identify. It may be so covered in other stuff that I will not be able to see it. And I have to ask—what if this is not the last time? What if it keeps happening?

I worry about all of this for my kids, so I take them away for the day, out of sight of the crime scene tape and the TV cameras. I leave for my own sake as well, to try and find a little space to reflect. And I leave because I can. Staying has always been a choice. The longer I stay, the less it feels like a choice, but that feeling masks the reality that I can move. I have the social capital, the education, the support network, and the financial equity that I can make a change if I want to. In a neighborhood starved for opportunity, the opportunity—the privilege—to start again belongs to me. It may not be easy, but I would certainly find a soft landing place. Few, if any, of my neighbors have that same opportunity.

Leaving is possible. We could go and start somewhere else. But leaving has consequences. Fleeing to a safer, whiter part of town would give us the illusion of suffering less. But it would come at a cost. The most immediate cost would be the loss of the daily joys that are part of Enderly Park. The music of the streets. The knocks on the door. The shouts of children at play.

The deeper layers of loss, beyond the change in our daily soundtrack, would be the way that the songs we hear and the songs we sing along Tuckaseegee are shifting the terrain of our souls. Years of listening, of repenting, of sitting on ash heaps with people I love, are transforming me. That is only possible through suffering. The avoidance of suffering is the avoidance of transformation. Walking away might protect our hearts, but it could also costs us our souls. To be transformed requires a long, patient struggle, full of suffering, watered with many tears.

I choose not to leave—and I do not want to leave—because I recognize that I need to be changed. I gain something from staying, something I need, something that I would not find anywhere else. Like Jacob, having forded the Jabbok river, I have strangers to wrestle through long nights like the one following Keith's death. One of those strangers is my own soul, which has been deadened by privilege, weakened by paths with too little resistance. In the story of his grappling with the divine stranger, Jacob wrestles all night and refuses to let go. Even through the deepest hours of darkness, just before the dawn, he keeps holding on until the stranger offers him a blessing. As the day is breaking, he finally walks away limping from his encounter, but also changed.[2]

Standing in that hotel pool, I think of my children growing up on Tuckaseegee. They will have to suffer, too, for my choices. They already have. The transformation possible through facing down the demons of the society they are growing up in—the ones that rob kids of opportunity, that accept the deaths of children as acts of obeisance to false gods, that claim the name of Jesus in public and then vote against his people by their policies—and of facing down those demons living in us makes the suffering worth it. I am willing to wrestle through that suffering, and I am willing to let my children do the same. I will not build protective blinders around their hearts only to jeopardize their souls. And I will not deny them the love their neighbors give—Jimmy's goofy humor, Ronnie's boisterous play, Antonio's absolute protection of them, Anthony giving them his last five dollars for their birthdays—in order to grant them the illusion of safety.

And standing in that hotel pool, I think of the kids who I did not bring with me. The ones who were at the scene. The one who came to tell me. The ones who heard the shots and the sirens and the noise of the crowd. Those kids and I climbed together, on that first day of summer camp nearly five years before, to the peak of Lover's Leap, gazing in silence across the hulking shoulders of mountains draining down to the French Broad River. If we can conquer mountaintops together, then so can we walk valleys with one another. Surely, as we walk through valleys of the shadow of death, we must keep walking together.

And so, the little boys and I dry off. I hug them, a little too tight, and we head back to Enderly Park.

I am not the first one to refuse to let go of an ache that will not leave, nor do I feel it the most deeply. For all the hurt of burying young people I have loved, I am neither their parent nor their sibling. The undertow of

2. Genesis 32:22-32.

grief feels like it may have pulled me under at times. For those family losing a beloved one, the current surely runs deeper and faster, beyond what I can conceive or imagine.

The blues are born from deep, troubled waters. The bluesmen and women held onto aches that would not leave. In "Backwater Blues," Bessie Smith, known to her audience in the 1920s and thirties as the "Empress of the Blues," sings of a fierce storm that sweeps away her house. After being rescued, she goes up on a hill above town to look down on what has been lost. The listener understands she is examining not only the lowlands from where she has been rescued, but also her grief itself. Her song, a classic of the blues tradition, reckons with both the storm and the deluge of sadness that follows the storm. One can hear in Smith's plaintive singing a song that resonates from the deep well of lament. Her voice cries from an ancient tradition of asking questions that do not have answers. She, like artists and singers and poets before her, sits alone and searches out words and sounds that can express the chaos below. Smith's story of loss and the deep but compact observations that follow never aim for resolve or rush to healing. It makes plain the loss, the effect of the loss, and the loneliness of observing the loss. To sing in such a way, and to refuse to be silent, offers a gift to all those who search for songs to sing as the currents of grief threaten to sweep them away.

The psalmists sing such songs as well. From the depths of troubled waters, one sings,

> Save me, O God
>> For the waters have come up to my neck.
> I sink in deep mire,
>> Where there is no foothold;
> I have come into deep waters,
>> and the flood sweeps over me.[3]

The lament psalms speak from floods of grief. The psalmists refuse to be silent in times of trauma and devastation. Rather than passive acceptance, they make demands on God to do something about grief and its source. God can and should act in response to injustice, the poet assumes, but seems to be asleep (as in Ps 44:23) or looking in another direction (as in Psalm 10:1).

---

3. Psalm 69:1–2.

Psalm 13 is a typical example. In only a few verses, the singer states her complaint to God, issues a plea or a command to God for help, and then makes a statement of trust in God's steadfast love. Like Bessie Smith, the psalm does not require lots of words to paint a picture of deep pain. A short question immediately cuts to the center in verse one: "How long, O Lord? Will you forget me forever?" The questions continue, followed by a command given to God: "Listen to me!" The sleeping God has to get woke in order to bring justice to places of injustice. The faithful pressure and implore God to remember that God's role in the world is to act in such situations.

The bold questions and commands of lament are typically followed by a confession of trust and a prayer of gratitude for the redemption that surely is to follow. The musicians singing psalms of lament hope that God will indeed awake and will act. Lament may serve as an effective protest that petitions God to become active. You don't protest the inactions of a God you don't believe can change, or can change things. In the lament psalms, God has fallen asleep.[4] It is the responsibility of the faithful to get God woke by their songs, by the prayers of their mouths and the prayers of their feet. Sitting on a high hill to observe loss and grief, and then responding with song that demands justice and waits in hope, is at the heart of the life of faith.

The New Testament has stories within the tradition of lament as well. One such story tells of Jesus and his followers sailing across the Sea of Galilee. After a long day of teaching, Jesus is tired and falls asleep in the boat. When a fierce storm blows up, the disciples fear for their lives. Waves are crashing over the side of the boat. The wind is piercing their bodies. The disciples are pretty sure that Jesus, who remains asleep through the storm, has brought them out on the water to die.

They begin yelling over the storm the questions of lament that the elders of their tradition have taught them: "How long are you going to let this go on? Why are you OK with our deaths? Do you not care that we are perishing?"[5]

Their lament works. They rouse the sleeping God, who acts on their behalf. Jesus gets up and speaks to the sea. In a moment, the storm stops raging and the sea is smooth as glass. The disciples react with awe at the mystery of the One who has displayed such power over the untameable sea.

4. Balentine, *Prayer*, 146–98, and Brueggemann, *Psalms*, 98–111.

5. Mark 4:35–41.

In the depths of their fear they cry out. Jesus acts during their moment of crisis, deepening their plunge into life with him.

Most of the lament psalms evoke this sort of story. They express dynamic, mature faith that depends on two-way interactions with a dynamic, relational God. They make statements of faith in a God who will act, even though the present circumstances may seem impossible. Even stronger, they make demands on a God who may have forgotten the covenant with God's people, and who may have fallen asleep at the helm, and needs to get woke before the ship runs aground.

But one psalm does not move to trust or hope. Psalm 88 breaks the form. It leaves open the possibility that some darkness may not have an answer. Some pleas for help may only fall into the abyss. Three times the poet cries out.[6] Three times the echo bounces back unanswered. Instead of a ray of hope, there is darkness.[7] The flood of grief, the deluge of God's wrath, closes in from every side. Finally the poet gives in to the waters of grief and submits to the darkness of the deep.

Sometimes there is no resolution, either internally or out in the world. The blues may come to rest in a place or on a person and just not leave. Even in times of ecstasy, like Bessie Smith at the height of an impassioned song, the blue notes still resonate. They touch deep within, in places that remain tender and unhealed. The blue notes give voice to the prayers that have gone unanswered, or the ones that cannot be answered, or the ones spoken to the sleeping God who did not awaken. But like the bleakest of the psalms, the prayer that cannot be answered must be prayed anyway. The song that ends without a resolution must be sung anyway. To sing or pray in this way is an essential move towards healing, if it is to come—and it may not. But you do not play the blues or pray a lament because you know you will get a certain response. You do it because in a world of hurt and injustice, there is no other song to sing and no other prayer to pray.

The blues keep coming back. The aches linger. A song may make the ache somewhat easier to bear, but no amount of singing the "Backwater Blues" brought Bessie Smith's house back. And no prayer has put Keith back on the streets among us. Out there remains a sister, a brother, a grandmother, and a growing child who still long for him to be there, and a whole bunch of others who get lost sometimes thinking about him.

6. Psalm 88:2, 9, 13.
7. Psalm 88:6, 12, 18.

The plain truth is that there are some young men whose lives I would have grieved as deeply as I grieved Keith's, but whose deaths would have been far less surprising. Some of the people I have been privileged to love, and who have loved me in return, move in dangerous circles where violence is not uncommon. Their deaths would have been no less tragic or heartbreaking, but they would not have had the same element of disbelief. But Keith was doing everything he was supposed to do, according to the script that society says should have helped him to move up in the world. He worked a job he loved that afforded him the opportunity to demonstrate his gentleness to children. He worked another job he only tolerated, but he did it to save money for the baby he was expecting, the one who had stolen his heart before she even arrived. He had furthered his education. And he was working at getting in shape, having changed some bad habits for better health. Things were going as well for him as could be expected, maybe better than could be expected given the difficulty of accessing opportunity in Enderly Park. One moment of cruelty stole all of that.

Each February since his death in 2013, a small memorial shows up at the corner where Keith died. Typically, it consists of a small bouquet of silk flowers, since live ones will not last long in midwinter. They remain until the power company comes in spring to cut the grass under the huge power poles that make up the skyline of Enderly Park. Keith's family builds an altar for him. Building altars is an ancient practice of remembering. In the place where something significant has happened, people put something in the ground—perhaps a tree, a flag, an obelisk, an arch. Maybe silk flowers, or a pile of stones, or a plaque.

Sometimes a marker gets improvised with whatever material becomes available. One fun diversion of city life is the installation of new sidewalks. Where concrete goes down to replace a cracked square, a group of people will show up just minutes after the work crew leaves. They memorialize themselves and their loved ones in the wet concrete. Decades from now, after a generation of gentrifiers has come and then gone on in search of more profitable pastures, folks will still read the names of D-Low, J-Rock, Squeaky, Ladybug, and Gina while they walk to the corner store. So will they see wishes to Khalil to rest in peace, in at least four places. This gives me great delight.

The ancestors did the same. Concrete is but manufactured stone, and the ancestors used stone, too, to mark places. When Jacob had a mystical experience in the wilderness, he moved a rock and then stained it to mark the spot where his dream ushered him into the presence of God. He called the place "God's House" to testify to its significance to him and to his descendants.[8] When the people Israel, named for their ancestor Jacob, finally defeated their long-time rivals the Philistines, they left a stone in the place of their deliverance and called it Ebenezer, meaning "thus far the Lord has helped us."[9] Leaving stories in the ground and etched into rock serves those who come behind by marking out spaces of remembrance. Wind and rain will one day rub surfaces smooth and ruin silk flowers, but not before the stories of the people and their place get told.

In 2015, a construction crew shows up at the corner of Tuck and Parkway. They dig down deep into the ground. All sorts of stories live in those layers of soil and clay. The crew has come today to mark one of those stories. Into the hole they excavate, the crew places a pewter-colored plaque embossed with black letters. It is a historical marker, one of the sort common on roadsides around the country marking a significant event or a person of interest to that particular place. The plaque marks only a single story, one that is not expansive enough for the many layers of soil and dirt they are digging through. In a spot that looks otherwise unremarkable, the sign commemorates S. B. Alexander. Below his name, the text reads, "First president of N.C. Farmers' Alliance, 1887. Was N.C. senator & U.S. congressman. Advocate of agricultural education. Home is 1 block S.E."

S. B. Alexander came from a notable clan in Charlotte history. Syd, as he was called, was born into a family of enslavers at Rosedale Plantation, an estate just north of downtown that now serves as a historic site and event venue. The Alexander family was local nobility. Streets, buildings, and other markers bear the family's name to this day. Syd used his family's prominence to make a name for himself in local politics. He eventually worked his way up to two terms in the United States House of Representatives.

Through the late 1800s and early 1900s, the west-side neighborhood now known as Enderly Park was simply "Enderly," the country estate of Sydenham Benoni Alexander.[10] At his farmhouse, he could relax at a

8. Genesis 28:10–22.

9. 1 Samuel 7:12.

10. Biographical information on S. B. Alexander comes from Noblin, "Sydenham Benoni Alexander." Further resources are available at "Sydenham Benoni Alexander," *Biographical Dictionary of US Congress*.

comfortable distance from the growing city of Charlotte. Separated from the bustle of town by two hills, with two creeks in between, he could stretch, take in the quiet, and work his farm. The latter of these was especially important to him. Alexander was notable in part for his agricultural activism. As a researcher, writer, and supporter of scientific agriculture, he made a career as farmer-scholar, a position in society lost in our day, but of high esteem in his.

In 1906, Syd moved from Enderly to Charlotte. The Alexander family maintained Enderly, and following his death in 1921, his daughter Julia lived at Enderly for several years. Midway through the 1920s, Julia determined that she would sell the land, and have it subdivided and parcelled out as a new neighborhood. Charlotte was growing out, moving across the second creek and up the hill. Enderly was to become Enderly Park, a new neighborhood on the outskirts of a growing city.

Julia Alexander was a champion of a number of progressive causes in her day. She was only the second female granted admittance to the North Carolina Bar, and she used her prominence to advocate for a number of issues that would improve life in Charlotte. One cause Julia Alexander took on was influencing Charlotte's urban development. She wanted to use Enderly as a living example of how the city as a whole, which was growing quickly, might develop into a livable, connected place. She contracted with John Nolen, a nationally prominent landscape architect and urban designer, to design the new neighborhood. Nolen was the founding president of the American Planning Association, and a visionary in city planning known around the country. His vision for Charlotte as a whole was to build in ways that incorporated the city's many creeks into a series of connected greenways. In his idea, neighborhoods would develop in relationship to one another in the manner in which the watersheds of the region naturally connected them. Enderly Park would become a living example of his ideal. Julia Alexander pushed this idea, but it turned out to be too far-sighted for the city at the time.[11]

Long, curving streets survive from Nolen's plan for Enderly Park, but the neighborhood is far less dense and internally connected than his

---

11. Kratt and Hanchett, *Legacy*, 124–25. Much of the history of the development of Enderly Park recounted here is drawn from this resource. Also, it is worth noting that the current trend of city planning and development in Charlotte is quite similar to John Nolen's ideas for the city in the 1920s. New growth often uses greenways to encourage connectivity along the natural geography of the landscape, and highlights the natural resources common in the area.

vision called for. A modest stone entrance stands along Tuckaseegee Road today to mark out an entrance to the neighborhood. The first houses were fine ones. They were not extravagant, as in the crosstown neighborhood of Myers Park, also designed by John Nolen. But the houses were large for their day, and handsome. Timing is everything in real estate, though, and those first houses were built from 1925–28. In 1929, the national economy collapsed. When the economy finally regained some health more than a decade later, building restarted. The dwellings that filled out Enderly Park reflected their construction in a leaner time. The shape of the neighborhood, including its lack of urban density, reflects still the inability of city elders to adopt the bold and progressive plan put forward by John Nolen and Julia Alexander for Charlotte's growth.

The marker for S. B. Alexander scratches the surface of this history, but it leaves out a number of important things. Syd Alexander was known to be a champion of several progressive causes in his day, including as an advocate for public education. He was instrumental in the establishment of a land grant university in the Raleigh area for the study of agriculture and the dissemination of advancements in mechanical and scientific agricultural techniques. North Carolina State University, as it would eventually be called, was an essential part of the education system of a growing state. But it used public resources in ways that benefited exclusively white students. The first Black students would not be admitted to NC State until 1953.

The plaque also leaves out Alexander's political affiliation. Alexander made his political career as a member of the Democratic Party. He was prominent during the period following Reconstruction. During the Post-Reconstruction era in North Carolina politics, so-called "Redeemer Democrats" ran on platforms aimed at reversing the progress of the Reconstruction period.[12] One of their concerns was the voting rights of Black and poor white voters, which Democrats perceived as a threat to white interests in the state. In the state-wide election of 1894, an alliance of Republican and Populist party voters elected a new majority into the state General Assembly, along with a Republican governor, the majority of seats in the state Supreme Court, and a majority of North Carolina's seats in the U.S. Congress.[13] Their success earned them the label "Fusion," meant derisively by Democrats. Over the next several years, and the next several elections, the Fusionists worked on a platform of voting rights, strengthening pub-

12. Durden, "Redeemer Democrats," 953.
13. Hunt, "Fusion of Republicans and Populists," 487–88.

lic schools, and handing local government control to local people. By the election of 1900, though, Democrats were back in control, chiefly by using race as a wedge issue to divide white voters from the "Fusion" alliance of Republicans and Populists. Once back in legislative power, the Democrats established Jim Crow rule in North Carolina, and disenfranchised Black voters again. S. B. Alexander was elected to office every two years during the period of the Redeemer Democrats from 1883 until 1894. In 1894, the Fusion alliance swept into power, and Alexander's term in office came, temporarily, to an end. When the Fusion alliance was finally broken in 1900, Alexander was again elected to the General Assembly, serving his final term in 1901–1902. Though the historical record on Alexander is a bit scarce, his electorate clearly saw him as aligned with the interests of the Democrats during his time.

Also left out of the plaque commemorating S. B. Alexander is the fact that he enlisted in the Confederate Army during the Civil War. He joined as fighting began the spring after he graduated from the University of North Carolina in 1860. While fighting for the Confederacy, he rose to the rank of captain. As an enlisted man rising through the ranks of the Confederate army, Alexander was willing to kill other humans to preserve the system of slavery that he had grown up benefitting from on Rosedale Plantation. This is the plain meaning of joining the Confederate army.

The geography of the marker in the ground for S. B. Alexander is important, so I should make it plain. On one side of Tuckaseegee Road, Khalil leaned against a fence and breathed his last breaths. On the other side of the street, in the place where Keith broke up the fight at the vigil, stands a memorial—an altar of civil religion—to a man who was willing to kill to keep Khalil's ancestors enslaved. The marker hides that important part of S. B. Alexander's story. It ignores that he sided with the Democrats in the establishment of Jim Crow, rather than with the multiracial Fusion movement. It buries into the ground parts of the story that must be uprooted and held up to the light in order to show people and places clearly and truthfully. Those hard parts of the story have to be named. Without naming and interrogating the hard truths of the past, there is no way to get free in the present. The hard parts of the story are the ones about which there can be no more silence.

It matters to whom society erects markers. It also matters to whom society does not erect them. There are many stories that remain in the ground that need telling. Every Charlotte neighborhood could have a marker for the Catawba people who occupied this land long before European settlers arrived. There are untold narratives of people who worked to build spaces of justice and kindness in the midst of a cruel society. There are movements that sprang up across the country to work for freedom and equality. In North Carolina, Fusion politics was one such movement whose members occupy little to no space in the historical consciousness of North Carolinians.[14] The story of the Fusion party, their successes, their legacy, and the strategies of racial fear and division used to put an end to the party are not well known among young people learning history. In my youth, I never learned of this hopeful movement within my state's politics. It matters that so many hopeful and compelling stories, like the history of the Fusionists in the late 1800s, remain concealed. They are hidden in the ground, while monuments to the Confederate dead occupy prominent locations in public spaces, and so also in imaginations.

The streets have a way of remembering, though, with or without official signs. Against the backdrop of the white fence at Tuck and Parkway, the initial memorial for Khalil remained in place for nearly two years. The little stuffed animals and bouquets of artificial flowers that marked the place from the awful August day forward were in terrible shape. They were beaten down by the weather, but no one could bear to remove them. Rain and sun erased the messages on the fence. Helms would leave paint pens and Sharpies out on occasion, as the love notes faded. The writing tools would need no explanation. The fence would fill back up in a day or two.

Other ways of remembering keep springing up. Street artists create memorials on blank walls, turning an unused canvas into a beautiful marker for beloved people. Folks in Enderly Park make T-shirts bearing the likenesses of loved ones, with slogans to their memory. We still have keychains imprinted with a picture of Keith, a short poem, and his birth and death dates. The departed here will be remembered, with or without the aid of archivists and history books.

These days the memorials for Khalil are not ever-present, but they reappear at least twice each year. Some token is placed in January at Khalil's birthday. And each August 14, flowers and balloons again mark the corner. A banner is hung on the fence. A small crowd gathers, and together we

---

14. Rev. Dr. William Barber and the Moral Mondays movement are doing good work in reviving this bit of history from North Carolina, and using it to set the narrative for the next era of North Carolina's history and politics. See Barber, *The Third Reconstruction*.

remember. We improvise a liturgy of remembrance with stories and laughs and passing the peace by hugs. Tears reconsecrate the ground. We mark the space once more as a sacred spot, holding within it a set of memories that have a hold of us. A space so marked has an effect on our bodies. I walk by this corner every single day. I know each time, usually consciously, but not always, that this space is "holy, though I knew it not."[15] Like Jacob, we have discovered another reason for the holiness of this ground, and so we charge the rocks and soil there with meaning.

Timing is as important in real estate as location is. Julia Alexander's plan for Enderly was never realized fully, in part because of bad timing. Between the Depression, the timidity of city leadership in Charlotte, World War II, and the explosion of automobile ownership and the building of superhighways, the late 1920s turned out to be a lousy time to build an urban neighborhood. By the time all the lots were sold and all the houses built, it was the mid-1950s. The changes of urban renewal and white flight in Charlotte were only a decade away. But by 2015 in Enderly Park, when the marker for S. B. Alexander went up, the real estate market had changed considerably. After decades of disinvestment from either municipal or private sources, Enderly Park and the neighborhoods around us were becoming fashionable again.

Historical markers can represent multiple layers of meaning. They can point out that even in common, overlooked places, important things happen, things that ought to be remembered. They can serve to engage the interests of people who see them. I am certainly an example of that—I knew nothing of S. B. Alexander before that sign went up.[16]

But signs can have another meaning as well. Though I am sure the timing of the placement of the Alexander marker was purely coincidental, it took place as the first moves toward displacement of the Black people of Enderly Park, and especially poor Black people, were happening. That timing is important. The sign has the appearance within the neighborhood of a marker that signals a coming change. The change is the reclaiming of land. The sign indicates that this space is going to be retaken by those to whom it did not rightly belong, which of course did not stop them from taking it the first time they took it. Read that way, the sign is consistent with

15. Genesis 28:10–22.

16. Thanks to Dr. Tom Hanchett for pushing me to think more thoroughly about the meanings of public markers.

the legacy of how land was apportioned when Enderly, the farm, became Enderly Park, the neighborhood. At that time the deed of sale read, in part, "lots of land shall be used for residential purposes only and shall be owned and occupied by members of the white race only." Enderly Park was legally established as segregated, white space. And though that language in the deed—which still exists—is not legally enforceable today, and has not been for some time, it is a potent reminder of how this place came to be.

The reclamation of Enderly Park by white folks will be legal, but it will not be just. It will be filed on the appropriate forms and placed in the appropriate drawers in a clerk's office downtown. But those forms will not account for the damage to children and families, or the networks of mutual aid that will be severed in the process, or the way that the displacement of cultural expressions and connections will isolate the long-time residents who manage to be able to stay. The historical marker cannot accomplish displacement and segregation, but it serves as a reminder to those with eyes to see that this is precisely what is happening. The sign is an eviction notice. The lease on the neighborhood is being terminated by a cruel and whimsical landlord who never allows his tenants to settle fully into a place.

The marker for S. B. Alexander places again into the ground the claim that some folks belong here and others do not. And those who will not belong here have never belonged here or anywhere, since they were ripped from their ancestral homes. They are always being displaced into the next undesirable place.

I trust that there is another story that will stay in the ground here. Even when Enderly Park is just another high-rent district, the church a microbrewery and the modest houses replaced with mansions, the streets will find a way to keep alive the memories of Khalil, and Keith, and Travis, and Lamont, those we have lost on this sacred soil. Grief gets planted in the ground as a story that persists in a place. Grief gets no triumphant sign or official recognition, but quietly, it remains. It keeps its hold, because grief grows from love. Love spreads underground through little rhizomes and pops up through cracks in sidewalks. Love does that, transforming grief by occupying dry valleys. It turns deserted places into gardens. And at the sight of it, the legs paralyzed by the weight of loss begin to find their footing again. The eyes blurred with tears see the light again. The soil built by love and watered with tears calls for returning, not all the time, but in rhythm. The sound of being called to turn around, to return to a place like home, fills the heart with gratitude for belonging. The call moves a person to again fill that space, and to be filled by it.

⌁

I watch from the front yard as Victor disappears behind the abandoned house at the curve. He does not reappear for a while. Another man follows him a couple minutes later, and also stays gone. Must be trouble, one assumes, given all the negative assumptions about this neck of the woods. Some illicit activity is going on—drug deals, probably, or perhaps just some guys hanging out, playing dominoes and wasting their days away.

A few weeks later, Victor and I are walking together to make a visit to a neighbor. As we round that same curve, he says, "Come on, let's take the cut." Behind the abandoned house we go, towards a small thicket. As we near it, I begin to see a well-worn path cutting through the thicket, underneath the old oak trees. The leaves have been swept away by footsteps, so that the path emerges—a thin line of Carolina red clay. A few steps later we are in the backyard of the matriarch of the neighborhood. We traverse her property line with great care, trying to match the care she has shown to multiple generations of children and parents here. She lives on the next street over, and now we have moved quickly and efficiently onto her street to visit with the family next door to her. "The cut" is simply a shortcut. It saves us a quarter mile of traversing our neighborhood's uneven street network.

Not too long after that walk, a couple of youth introduce me to another cut. We're out on a warm spring day, but the weather has not yet been warm long enough for the kudzu to spread. We head to the dead end of a particular street, where they show me yet another thin line of Carolina clay. To the right, a long hill descends to a stream. Opportunistic kudzu vines occupy every available space between us and the water. The power company keeps the hill covered in vines, rather than trees, to provide clearance. To the left, an older neighbor waves to us from his porch, his watchful eye noting who comes and goes. He is quickly out of sight, separated from us by a thicket that will become forest if left alone for much longer. As we round the bend, with kudzu on one side and the tangle of bushes and vines on the other, our destination comes into view: Cook-Out, the local burger and shakes chain, stands flanked by our mechanic and a small grocer.

The youth show me the way but offer an important tip—no one uses this cut during the summer. It gets too overgrown with kudzu. The fear of ticks and snakes and creeping, crawling things makes the long way more attractive. But with the first frost, the kudzu gives way again to the rusty orange path. The critters go underground. The dead end street begins to make connections once more.

In Charlotte, like many other Southern cities, neighborhoods do not always have urban form. They are not densely built or easy to walk. The automobile dominance that characterized the time of rapid growth here led to neighborhoods that do not connect, either to other neighborhoods, or even within themselves. Covering a short distance "as the crow flies," as we say in the South, to a neighbor's house or to the corner store, can require a lengthy walk. With time, as neighbors develop intimacy with the places that become home turf, they can imagine how to make these connections for themselves where planners and builders have failed them. And so they do, mingling private and public space, reclaiming dead places and making them human again.

Cities and towns like Charlotte built neighborhoods that made human connection difficult without the assistance of an automobile. Long blocks, lack of a simple street grid, separation of uses, ever-larger lots, lack of sidewalks, and emphasis on single-family housing rather than a mix of housing and commercial types characterize these towns and cities. All of those physical characteristics create spaces that put people at greater distance from one another. In the 1960s and '70s, as middle-class people moved from older neighborhoods, out into even less-connected subdivisions, the poor were left to occupy spaces where infrastructure stifled connection. Connection is the currency that keeps the economy of urban life flowing. So, the so-called "inner-cities" of Charlotte got double bad news with "white flight"—all of the negative policy and disinvestment decisions that made inner-city life tough around the country, and none of the diverse, walkable, human-powered infrastructure that facilitates the creative vibrancy and opportunity of urban spaces.

Facing these significant barriers, poor people did what they always do in the face of oppressive circumstances. They acted with imagination, creativity, and resilience to create what they needed for human life. The cut is do-it-yourself urbanism. It is the resilient human spirit finding ways to build connection where planners and councils and developers failed to deliver. The cut is what happens when people who have always had to improvise look at what is given and use their imaginations to improve it.

In Enderly Park, those cuts and the neighbors who introduced them to me have helped to nurture my sense of neighborliness. How long those neighbors will remain is in question, as speculators are circling. The imaginative, improvisational folks that have lived here for decades are being banished. They are deemed hazardous to profit margins, and must be displaced to other parts of town. Among the collateral damage of this kind of neighborhood change is the cut. Our cuts are being blocked by a new feature—fences.

Like historical markers, or deeds, or flags, fences are used to mark out and claim space. This can be very helpful. Good fences make good neighbors, they say. But what constitutes a good fence? What shape does a good fence come in? How tall is it and what is it made of? Where are the gates, and who gets to use them?

As new, upwardly-mobile people—most of them white—move in, more and more privacy fences go up. They are tall fences that cannot be seen through at all. A simple chain link may lack in aesthetic appeal, but it does the job of keeping toddlers in a safe space. It also makes a good trellis. Neighbors can grow blackberries on them, and talk as they pick the fruit from either side. Chain link does not inhibit conversation. But the six-foot privacy fence that is becoming more common now does something different. It is not permeable. The flower beds behind it can only be enjoyed by one or two sets of eyes. The kids restricted within it cannot find other kids, and cannot help break the ice between the adults that belong to them.

The new neighbors moving to Enderly Park build these privacy fences really well, and thoroughly. Most everybody moving in gets one. And so one day everyone will be cut off from one another. The lessons of improvised urbanism are being replaced by the assertion of private property rights and the false assumption that a few pickets around a yard can protect people from each other. The poor people and children who build cuts are neighborhood visionaries. They challenge the middle-class affinity towards individualism, toward the belief that one's property is an inviolable castle. Poor folks build the infrastructure for solidarity. The cut is what happens when you know that private interests are deeply commingled with the good of the whole neighborhood. This knowledge lives in the ground in Enderly Park. It is not taught, but caught, by walking in the steps your neighbor walked before you, that your children will walk after you. Neighborliness is a quiet inheritance in this way. It gets passed up through the soles of your shoes and takes root in your heart and eyes.

In winter, the rust-colored path reveals itself once more. My walk to the grocery is a bit shorter, and on it I bump into a neighbor. Amid the sprawl of receding vines, we talk—kids, work, local politics, what's for supper. The things of life. I do not know that I need this conversation until it happens, and I feel my shoulders softening, as well as my soul with them. I need to walk this way again. As walls and fences and borders come to define more places, secret, unmapped spaces that defy those boundaries will multiply, and the more our souls will need to seek them out.

Ready to move again, the narrow cut forces us to touch one another. We brush shoulders. We bump hands. What might it be like, I wonder, if lives were built like this kudzu hill: covered in wild connections, as far as the eye can see; quietly observing seasons of growth and rest; sometimes revealing paths for gently brushing against one another?

To the untrained eye, it is obvious that fences are in a season of growth. But on a quiet winter day, I can imagine that we are more creative than fences. That we still need to run into each other. That there are more cuts to build across the landscapes of our neighborhoods and the terrain of our hearts. That we will still find new ways of getting to our neighbor's door.

⌁

One of the cardinal rules of youth ministry is that you cannot have favorites. So I am not saying that Alicia is one of my favorites. But she does take over the room with her abundance of gifts. Chief among those gifts is a fire in her belly for seeing things made right. She will not tolerate an injustice when she sees it, no matter how small, and she will tell an offender exactly what she thinks of them and their actions. Alicia also transforms that indignation easily into compassion for someone who has been injured or harmed. She is fierce and gentle in equal measure. She naturally brings others in, nurturing those who would be forgotten.

Alicia's mother has told her for her whole life that her name (her real name) means "warrior princess." That name is just right for Alicia—strong, loyal, and fierce. You would want her on your side in battle. She is also extravagant. Not in material wealth, but in hospitality and kindness. From the abundance of feeling within her, she gives.

Alicia has another gift. It is a gift for words. She tried to write a novel once, and was making good progress before the challenges of school assignments derailed her. Alicia's gift with words is not in writing lots of them, though. It is in getting to the heart of the matter. She can take a difficult or complex subject, especially an emotionally complicated one, and distill it down to a root problem quickly and elegantly.

Alicia can do this in formal language, words of the sort that have her on a path to graduating from college and moving out into the world to put her gifts to use in solving difficult problems. She can also do this quickly and elegantly in the language of the streets.

Around Enderly Park, people often say "the streets talk." This truism is proven right over and over again. If you want some news to get out among the people, the informal channels are the most efficient way of doing that. When there is a piece of extra good gossip around the neighborhood, it coats the neighborhood as oil in a hot pan. If someone runs into trouble with the law, word sizzles through the streets. And when the community center hosts a cookout and rummage sale, the good news passes along without effort. Organizing an event or building a movement here requires knowing how to get the right messages into those channels in the right way. When the revolution comes, we will not need flyers for it on Tuckaseegee.

Not only do the streets talk, but the streets have their own lingo. Just like Black American music, the language that is shared among neighbors here is relentlessly inventive. Like an improviser with a horn, language is spoken in rhythm, in a way that is always open to the next surprise to come. At any moment, there may be a new color to enliven the topic, or a new way of shaping a phrase, or an innovation that allows the speaker to shift adroitly from one subject to another. The best improvisers roll with the surprises, always welcoming whatever gift may show up.

There is music in the language of the streets. Miles Davis, the great trumpeter and musical innovator, used to say that music is what happens between the notes. The language of the streets is like that—it distills, it dances around the edges, it flirts with listeners. People play with language like Miles played his trumpet—sometimes coy, sometimes bold and direct, sometimes darting in and out and through the words, but always pushing on the edges. Serious work happens in the space between the notes, the space between the words. Meaning is packed into small spaces.

Street talk is a way of knowing, a serious pursuit of giving verbal meaning to an embodied life lived in a world that does not make good sense.

Informal language is often looked down upon from lofty places. Places of privilege and prestige demand the formality and precision of certain modes of speech. Formal language is needed in certain contexts—surgery, maybe, or statecraft. But the language of the street captures meaning and turns of phrase that formalities cannot express. Life lacks clarity sometimes. Poetry and rap and the blues express the irony and imprecision and bluesy-ness of living. Verbal shortcuts get to the heart of the matter without lengthy explanations.

One of Alicia's gifts for language is her ability to capture ambiguity in a short phrase. She can get at the stuck places that make speech difficult. She enters into the wildness of her own experience and often manages to pull out a phrase or idea that penetrates the situation in just the right way. While Helms and I are working on a garden project with several youth one afternoon, she tells us about an organization she wants to start.

"I'm going to call it the 8-14-12 Foundation," she says.

Helms and I glance at each other. We know without speaking the significance of that number. It is the date Khalil died.

"What's your foundation going to do?" Helms asks.

"It is going to address youth violence."

"I love it, Alicia," Helms says. "What got you thinking about that?"

"It's just that after Khalil died, nobody did anything. And I don't think that's OK."

Nobody did anything, she said. Which nails it. She is voicing a lament, singing a blues. Alicia knows that the events that led to Khalil's death were not simply about youthful irresponsibility or unexplainable cruelty. They happened in a context, in a structure, in a society where the needless deaths of children have not spurred the collective resolve to change that society. Such death is merely a design feature at this point, just one of the ways things work. The ambiguous "nobody" she points the finger at is adults. They—really, we—are passing her a world fenced in and armed to the eyeballs. Neighbors are afraid of neighbors. The deaths of children on street corners and in schools, rather than being a call for self-reflection and sacrifice, has resulted in the hardness of hearts and increased sales at the gun shop. Those reactions are the reason that Alicia and her friends are "shut in so that they cannot escape."[17]

It is not the generic idea of "children" that Alicia is thinking about, though that ought to be enough. She is thinking of one child in particular.

17. Psalm 88:8.

Her lament is specific. She remembers the tears she shed on 8-14-12. She and her friends were overcome by them, standing on the corner with their tears "surrounding them like a flood all day long."[18] The feeling still hits her when she walks by. Not every time, but enough. To Alicia, knowing this feeling deeply is enough to open her imagination to what others in the same boat have walked through. The fire in her belly rises up. She must speak and act. Her whole being requires it of her.

Alicia's words get at the hole in language that the death of a child brings about. Kids dying defies grammar. Logic wilts in the heat of it. But her words, when they finally come, communicate something she knows deeply—that in Enderly Park, cruel conditions make children here more prone to suffering interpersonal and institutional violence than their peers almost anywhere else in the city. Those conditions were created and are maintained by powers beyond Alicia's reach. They are the direct result of deliberate public policy decisions made by people who do not have to live with the harshest consequences of those decisions. They will only be undone by deliberate decisions that finally take seriously the responsibility to every child to build the best possible streets in the best possible neighborhoods.

"No one did anything," she cries out. The world keeps spinning, but nobody is turning around. So she sings these blues, and refuses to be silent, and makes demands of the world. She makes demands of God. She is the voice crying out in the wilderness, the one who comes singing the ancient songs of the faithful.

18. Psalm 88:17.

7

In the Garden[1]

"A strange and bitter crop."[2]

OUR NEIGHBOR JEFF IS trying to teach us to be farmers. His syllabus boils down to this—start with the soil. Jeff's favorite technique for building soil is called *hugelkultur,* which I think is German for "act like a forest." Jeff says that to build a *hugelkultur* bed, you first outline the desired area with logs. Big, thick, heavy logs are best, from trunks and large branches. Next, lay down cardboard inside the outline to kill any grass and weeds. Grass is your new enemy, and you need to be ready for a long, bitter fight. Next, begin piling sticks, branches, twigs, leaves, wood chips, dirt, manure, and any other organic material you can find in it, mostly woody stuff. Pile it up. Then wet it. Water it frequently. And wait. Waiting is the thing you do the most of.

While you are waiting—months and months of waiting—the most amazing transformation is happening. After six months, maybe even a year, you stick your hand into the bed where there were sticks and leaves, and pull out handfuls of rich, black, damp soil. It is loose and loamy. Every speck is alive. Worms and bugs everywhere. You may find little earth snakes, which are like oversized worms. There are millions of microbes in every handful. The dead trees you were working with are alive again, and the only thing you did was put it all in a pile.

1. Holiday, "Strange Fruit." Simone, "Strange Fruit."
2. Allan, "Strange Fruit." Used by permission.

Jeff loves teaching people to do this. His lessons are about a technique that enables the midwifery of nurturing soil. Jeff also has a series of go-to questions that help give birth to an understanding of how the created world works. His questions go like this: Have you ever lived in or near the woods? If you did, did you ever have to water your woods? Did you ever need to fertilize your woods?

The answers to those last two questions, of course, are no. No one waters their stand of woods, even during the worst drought. Neither does anyone fertilize their woods. To have the woods closeby, you just stop tending to an area and wait. The forest will happen without you. In fact, the forest happens best without you. Sticks fall. Leaves drop. An ice storm prunes back unhealthy branches. Critters take refuge. Leave your yard or field alone, and the forest will *hugelkultur* it back into a fecund, nurturing environment. The forest creates a system that replicates itself in the absence of any interference.

When developers build new housing developments, it is common to remove all the evidence of the forest, save perhaps a few trees. Most of the trees, plus all the emerging undergrowth, animals, and edge plants marking the transition from field to forest are displaced. Well, the trees are killed, really, but because nature is more creative than housing developers, they will live on as mulch to nurture new growth. All of this destruction makes way for pavement, houses, and yards.

Once the forest is gone, the topsoil is removed. The forest has been building life by generating a couple of inches of topsoil every one thousand years or so. In a few hours, the topsoil that the ancient forest made, which kept remaking the forest, is loaded into a truck to be sold in plastic bags to big-box customers. This transformation is known by the names "progress" and "freedom."

The forest is now replaced with a lawn, which can be regulated, and is. The city and the homeowners' association demand that the lawn be cut. If trees remain, or are planted, their fallen leaves must be removed in a timely fashion so as to create a certain appearance. In the South, the new lawns are often sown with Bermuda grass, which is the horticultural equivalent of the mosquito. It thrives in marginal soil, hiding the damage of the opportunistic removal of topsoil. Bermuda spreads quickly by underground rhizomes, making it at the same time great for building a lawn and the bane of a Southern gardener's existence. The new lawn now needs feeding and watering. It requires cutting and trimming and the burning of fossil fuels by noisy engines. An inviting carpet of grass takes hours of care, plus a load of money.

Leave the grass uncut, though, and the forest will slowly begin again. The world that is to come will start, imperceptibly at first, to reclaim the lawn. Bird waste might plant and fertilize a seed that becomes a bush. Unraked leaves will rot. Wind-blown pods will sprout saplings that begin reaching for the sun. Creatures will find spots to nest. A lone hickory tree will use a forgetful squirrel to give birth to the next generation of hickory trees. A canopy will begin to form, shading out the Bermuda grass. A tree will fall and become a nurse log, nourishing the new world. Fruits and nuts will grow on the edges, inviting more life to find shelter. The forest re-establishes its system. The genius of this system is that it replicates itself. Once established, the forest produces all the material it needs to continue. It does this best without interference.

The genius of any system—whether forest, or political, or religious, or economic, or otherwise—lies in its ability to replicate itself. When the products are rich soil, homes for birds, nuts to eat, and air to breathe, this is a wonder. But if a system produces bad fruit, poisonous soil, and suffocating gases, problems happen. Without interference, such a system will eventually destroy almost everything around it. If you want a garden that thrives, one you can eat from and relax in, you have to create a system where everything, in life and in death, works together to make flourishing possible.

To show support for some crosstown friends and their daughter, Helms visited a middle school located near their home to cheer on the daughter in a softball game. When she arrived, the first thing she noticed was the grass. It really was greener on the other side of town. As she kept looking, she noted that the grass at this little field was not the only pristine thing about the facility. The whole place—field, stadium, dugouts, everything—was in immaculate shape. For a softball field at a public middle school, she thought this seemed a bit excessive. Between innings, she asked our friends about the facility, and learned that it was maintained by the parents of the athletes. They mowed the grass, painted the lines, and kept the equipment in good working order. They spent many hours and devoted lots of resources towards their children having one of the best facilities in the city in which to learn the disciplines of sport.

Helms saw clearly, and felt in her gut, a difference in this section of town from our home in West Charlotte. She and I have attended many middle-school sporting events to cheer for QC Family Tree youth, but those were several years prior. In 2010, the school board closed the three middle schools on our side of town. In a school system with more than thirty middle schools, only three were shuttered. All were in West Charlotte. The students in those schools were assigned to elementary schools that became K-8 programs. The new schools fielded few sporting teams, they had fewer arts resources, and extracurricular opportunities were scarce.

Helms could also see in her mind's eye the west-side high-school football field where our youth often practiced. The school had a proud winning tradition, but only marginal facilities. There were bald patches in the grass, rickety stands for spectators, and scoreboards that had clearly seen better days. The games were still a huge draw for the surrounding community, but there was a marked difference in the facilities. That difference has meaning. It did not—does not—go unnoticed.

We talked about the differences when she returned home from the softball game. We discussed how the parents who spent hours and hours on the fields for their children were to be commended for their dedication. Their commitments represented a system of family values that should be celebrated. Children ought to see people who love them working on their behalf to enrich the soil of the places where they grow up. A good ballfield for nurturing friendships seems like a fine way to do that.

But "family values" exist in a system—a set of coordinated components that produce particular results—that extends outside the foul lines. Those values are part of a system that is often overlooked and unnamed, but is there nonetheless. Systems work best in the background. A computer's operating system runs thousands of lines of code in the background to enable a user to send a single email. The cable system of a suspension bridge allows drivers to enjoy the view over the bay without worrying about plunging into the water. Systems, once started, disappear from sight and produce outcomes, but those outcomes are not always the desired ones. The best intentions of the designers will not cover for design flaws. Even worse is the system designed with bad intentions, the one that finds inequitable outcomes to be acceptable or even desirable.

The name for the system where wealthy white families with middle-school children have professional-quality ball fields while poor Black families do not even have middle schools is white supremacy. A system of supremacy, or domination, uses all the small components that comprise the system to produce particular outcomes. Those outcomes privilege certain members over others in the distribution of goods, and land, and power. In the system of white supremacy that has been part of United States history since the arrival of the first settlers here, those who receive the benefits are the ones declared to be "white." The definition of "white" changes over time, but those who are defined as white at some certain point in time receive privileges that are not universally available to their contemporaries. Probably the most prized of these is access to economic and political power. Being white does not guarantee wealth or prestige, but it puts the opportunity to become wealthy or prestigious closer at hand. In terms of social mobility, whiteness is one of the factors that makes moving up the ladder to the top 20 percent easier. And the opposite is true as well—being a person of color almost always means starting closer to the bottom, and having a harder time moving up across class lines.

Being born "white" does not guarantee wealth or good fortune. Neither does being born white in a system of white supremacy make one a Klan member or a Nazi by default. My friends and neighbors in the white, wealthy part of town are kind and decent people, especially the ones Helms went to the softball game with. They claim to care about the inequalities across our city. They love Jesus and devote many hours to service in their churches and to raising up their kids as disciples of Jesus. But no amount of good intentions or goodwill by any one person or group will guarantee good or equitable outcomes for every child. Systems replicate outcomes until they are taken apart and put back together differently. Simply cutting the grass less often at the fancy ball field will not bring the west-side middle schools back, nor the sports and music programs that went with them. Neither will claiming some distance from the domination system, or trying to escape complicity in it—the "Not all white people!" defense—change the nature of the system. Fruit grown in bad soil will not be good fruit, regardless of the intentions of the grower.

Charlotte, North Carolina, is producing a significant share of bad fruit from bad soil. In this, Charlotte is a reflection of U.S. culture, which contains the same base elements and gets roughly the same results. All of the metrics indicate this. Health outcomes, educational outcomes, judicial and penal-system outcomes, levels of generational wealth and net worth all show that people of color in Charlotte and across the nation are oppressed, underserved, disregarded, and ignored. This has always been the case. The soil where QC Family Tree is planted has not been healthy for a long time. Our trees have "blood at the root."[3]

Forests are complex systems that propagate themselves unless some other force interferes. This is the genius of a forest, which will always begin again the patient labor that produces one inch of humus every thousand years or so. But what about the forest that produces no fruit, or worse, the one that grows poison? What to do with a system that feeds children fruits that harm them? Or that eventually turns and devours itself? "Every tree that does not bear good fruit is cut down and thrown into the fire,"[4] John preaches in the wilderness. But even cutting down the edifices producing the worst fruit of American culture will not stop the systems from regrowing. To do that, the soil must be analyzed and tested. As farmer Jeff teaches, to grow good fruit you begin with good soil. One question to ask to understand the injustice in particular communities is, "What's in the ground?"

In the 1890s, Charlotte was a small city consisting primarily of what is called "Uptown" today. (In Charlotte, Uptown is just downtown gussied up.) The one square mile or so that comprised the city was surprisingly integrated. Records show that Black and white folks inhabited the same blocks, often living side by side, though in different economic conditions. The injustice of the race-based caste system was fully present, but also present was a complex enough set of relations that different folks could share the same ground. They could have yards bordering one another.

Proximity matters. It gives birth to imagination and possibilities that are not accessible without bodies bumping up against one another. On a block with a diversity of experiences and perspectives, it was easier, at least in theory, for folks to imagine that they had shared interests and could work for a common good. The work of imaginative solidarity was much harder for those in the dominant culture—the white people—but the design and architecture of the city made it a possibility.

This changed rapidly, within just a few years. As the Fusion politics of Republicans and Populists in North Carolina failed, in large part because of the exploitation of racial fear by white-supremacist Democrats, Charlotte

3. Allan, "Strange Fruit." Used by permission.
4. Matthew 3:10.

became "sorted out," or fully segregated by race.[5] By the first decade of the 1900s, much of the Black population of the city was confined to a couple of areas. One of those areas was the neighborhood called Second Ward. Residents of Second Ward took to calling their area "Brooklyn," because they were building it in the same urban fashion as Brooklyn, New York. (That borough of New York City is the most sought-after real estate in the country in the early twenty-first century, which will be important to this story later.) In an area of about sixty blocks, the people of Charlotte's Brooklyn built a thriving district, with high levels of Black ownership, and were creating the kind of neighborhood that fostered deep connections and nurtured strong community. They were self-determining, turning what could have been cause for despair into a thriving, resilient culture and flourishing district.

The thousands of residents there owned hundreds of businesses, went to churches they built themselves, worked in every possible profession, educated their children in schools they were proud of, built civic groups, cared for their sick, and funeralized their dead all within a few blocks. They did this in the face of white terrorism; without the aid of the Federal Housing Administration, which was at the same time helping white families build wealth through homeownership; without the assistance of the GI Bill for their young men returning from war; without Social Security available to many of their workers to help spread wealth across generations; without equal access to educational opportunity; and without equal protection under law. Brooklyn was a near-miracle, a triumph of will and persistence and ingenuity.

By the early 1960s, several generations had been raised in Brooklyn. Significant institutional and economic power had been built there out of nothing but work and mutual support. Brooklyn was thriving. But it was also strategically located, which meant that a new municipal project put it in jeopardy.

Rising Black economic and social power in the United States has almost always led to a backlash, usually one that is entirely legal and done with a smile. Economic development projects mean doom for Black communities, giving cover to systems of power to destroy those communities while claiming to be working for the public good. From the 1940s through the seventies, these sorts of projects were built through programs named "urban renewal." They destroyed thriving Black neighborhoods across the country: Union Hill in Richmond; Hayti in Durham; Brooklyn in Charlotte;

---

5. Hanchett, *Sorting Out the New South City*, 116–44.

and several hundred others, touching almost every medium to large city in the U.S.

In the 1960s and into the 1970s, Charlotte began to take funding from the federal government for urban renewal. This federal funding was aimed at "slum clearance." The funding authorized the city and the state to condemn and then destroy entire blocks, paying owners of a condemned property only a portion of its real value, in order to build mega-projects. Across the country, urban renewal projects were most often highways. In Charlotte, one of the largest projects was the construction of the downtown expressway loop.

The stated intentions of urban renewal in Charlotte, and of projects like it around the country, was to bring renewed life to center cities by making travel into those cities quicker for suburban residents coming to work. Renewing cities by destroying densely populated neighborhoods is curious logic. Planners failed to recognize that a quick way into downtown was also a quick way out of downtown, turning center city Charlotte into a ghost town after 5 p.m. By destroying viable downtown neighborhoods, and then offering downtown office workers a quick exit plan, urban renewal not only flattened the urban fabric of Charlotte, it encouraged and subsidized the rapid growth of suburban, car-dependent, hyper-segregated development.

The racial implications of urban renewal were plain to see, though they went unnamed by those pushing for the projects. Inevitably, urban highways were built through areas with large minority populations, or with high rates of poverty, or both. Government authorities, in meetings and forums and sometimes in backroom deals, would propose projects to remove "problem" neighborhoods. They would pass motions and policies to make the new projects a reality, and begin filing for eminent domain rights to seize property, paying small buyouts to property owners with no choice but to accept. Then bulldozers would appear to flatten neighborhoods, razing entire blocks to the ground in preparation for another project.

When Charlotte's Brooklyn was destroyed, it was home to more than a thousand families, two hundred businesses, several dozen churches, an important school, social clubs, restaurants, two movie theaters, and many other diverse uses. Today, there is almost no physical evidence it ever existed, except for a handful of buildings just far enough from the highway to survive the wrecking ball. And this is just one example of such a project in Charlotte. Other neighborhoods downtown, like Earle Village and

Woodlawn, plus an entire district through northwest Charlotte, suffered the same fate.

Calling these expressway construction projects "slum clearance" was the weaponization of language. Naming a neighborhood a slum purely along racial lines was the standard of the day, and the roots of that kind of language have not disappeared. The use of such language says more about the people doing the talking than it does about the condition of the neighborhoods being condemned and stolen. There is no question that there was not enough money in Brooklyn, or in most Black communities. Many people were poor. But destroying a neighborhood because of the presence of poor people is like treating a case of pneumonia by amputating all of the patient's limbs. The root of the poverty was the system of white supremacy, which went unaddressed then, and remains unaddressed now.

The poverty present in neighborhoods subjected to urban renewal around the country came about in an environment. It had a cause. A policy framework upheld the conditions. One does not have to dig far into the ground to find that the nutrients had been stripped from the soil by a series of decisions. Policies are law, or practices upheld by law. They are guidelines for governing the common life of the city. Policies are like the soil in a forest system. Good policy can produce good fruit, and bad policy will yield bad fruit.

Among the many layers of unjust policy that caused and maintained poverty in Black communities across the country was a practice known as redlining. The Federal Housing Administration (FHA), as part of the New Deal, backed many home loans. It still does. This federal intervention drove down the cost of borrowing money to levels that made home ownership practicable for millions of people who had never been able to afford to buy their houses. It did this by reducing the size of downpayment needed, and by reducing interest rates. For banks and lenders, FHA backing reduced their risk, thus making the lending of larger sums over longer periods of time more profitable and less risky.

However, the FHA upheld a series of policies that governed where and to whom FHA-backed loans were available. On maps, administrators drew lines around neighborhoods in a variety of colors. Blue and green lines indicated neighborhoods where these public funds were encouraged. Yellow lines indicated caution. Red lines indicated that the FHA would not back loans in those neighborhoods. Among the reasons that a neighborhood would be redlined was the presence of Black people. A single Black family, regardless of how wealthy they were, would downgrade a blue or green neighborhood immediately. If multiple Black families lived there, a neighborhood was considered to be in serious decline, and thus ineligible for the public subsidies being awarded to white neighborhoods.

The redlining maps in Charlotte show a pretty clear reality. Compare them with today's street map, and you can see a close correlation between redlined neighborhoods and the location of today's expressways. Which means that the federal government, as a standard practice beginning in the 1930s, withheld money in Black communities while giving it to white communities through wealth-building homeownership opportunities. Then, in the 1960s, the same governmental bodies condemned those Black communities, saying that they had the appearance of having too little wealth. Public policy created or worsened the conditions to cause poverty in some places, and then policymakers, with the support of white communities who voted for them, punished them for being poor.

This is not ancient history. Both redlining and urban renewal continued into the 1970s. Many of the people who were harmed by these practices are still alive.[6] People whose land was seized and whose businesses were destroyed are still active members of local communities, with stories to tell and voices to be heard. Though their neighborhoods cannot be rebuilt as they were, reparations can be made for the harm done. And, the same institutions that contributed to that harm—governmental bodies, corporations, nonprofits, churches, and so on—can examine the soil in which supremacist practices grew, work to uproot all of the trees that bear bad fruit, and to build the good, healthy soil native to their region.

⟐

In New York City, one of the neighborhoods hardest hit by redlining was Harlem. Billie Holiday moved there as a teen in the 1920s, prior to urban renewal, but the heat of racial oppression was already exerting white-hot pressure on neighbors. Of that same Harlem, a couple of decades later, Baldwin wrote to his nephew, "This innocent country set you down in a ghetto in which, in fact, it intended that you should perish."[7] Moving through oppressed spaces like Harlem as a child, and living with a mother who survived on the margins of society, Holiday knew Baldwin's words

6. One good introduction to this history is Coates, *We Were Eight Years*, 163–208.

7. Baldwin, *The Fire Next Time*, 7.

before he wrote them. She lived in rough conditions from the very beginning. She kept up the hard living until the very end, dying in 1959 at age 44.
Following an arrest on drug charges late in her life, Holiday found herself
in court on a case called "United States of America versus Billie Holiday."
Referring to the name of the case, she quipped, "And that's just the way it
felt."[8] She was not talking only about that court case.

Billie Holiday's most important song came from a collaboration with
the poet Abel Meeropol, who wrote under the pen name Lewis Allan. He
had written a poem called "Strange Fruit." Using images of the strange fruit
growing from trees in the agricultural South, he called attention to lynch-
ings there. The lyrics of the poem never used the word "lynching," but the
image was clear. The poem was lament. It was protest. It was rage. And it
needed a musical collaborator.

Meeropol found one in Billie Holiday. She was frightened of the song
at first, fearing a backlash from white listeners, reviewers, and record-label
executives. But despite taking withering criticism in the press, she per-
formed it anyway. And she kept performing it. Audiences demanded it. She
could not play a night without it. Years later, *Time* magazine, an initial critic
of the song, called it the most important song of the twentieth century.

Sometimes a song finds the right voice. So it was with Billie Holiday
and "Strange Fruit." This one woman, who in court had faced the weight
of the whole United States of America, gave voice to the terror Black folks
faced in the American domination system, and not just in the South. Her
voice communicates that terror. In recordings of the song, she sometimes
sounds weak with grief. At other points, she is alive with anger. She lingers
in just the right places. She cuts words short where the pain is too sharp.
And though she is young, she sounds weathered. Weary. Exhausted. And
at the same time, she is righteously enraged, and in full knowledge that the
battle is far from over.

Holiday knew that she had to keep singing this lament. It was difficult
for her to do. "It depresses me every time I sing it," she said. This was in
part because it reminded her how how her father died. A World War I vet,
he faced ongoing lung issues after being exposed to mustard gas. He died
in 1937 after being denied treatment at a hospital in Texas. Holiday also
knew that she had to keep singing "Strange Fruit" in part because of him.

---

8. Holiday, *Lady Sings the Blues*, 146.

"Twenty years after Pop died the things that killed him are still happening in the South," she said.[9]

⊕

What happens when the good soil gets stripped away? What comes next? In Charlotte's former Brooklyn neighborhood, the fruits of the bad soil are plain to see. There is a jail now. Where once homes stood to nurture Black children, now a jail warehouses hundreds of people, mostly Black and Latinx,[10] in a system of mass incarceration. This system destabilizes neighborhoods, destroys families, and wrecks the fragile economy of the disinherited.

Not only is there a jail, there are numerous parking lots. The basic calculation of urban renewal was that empty space was more beneficial than Black space. So, good soil got topped with pavement. Nothing grows in pavement. Presiding over this district of parking lots and government buildings is a church. The First Baptist Church of Charlotte, a Southern Baptist congregation, moved from their home on Charlotte's main street to a large new facility, with a tall steeple casting a long shadow over this twice-stolen land.

In 2017, architects and planners began to build out a new plan for Brooklyn. Parking lots and drab office buildings will be replaced with high-rise apartments, restaurants, beer gardens, lots of shops, a theater, and a Whole Foods. Fifty years after the destruction of the neighborhood, people will live there again. The land is worth millions of dollars, the new developments millions more. The buyouts offered to former residents when they were forced to leave pale in comparison to the current value. The people of Charlotte have another opportunity to reckon with the fact that by the force of the city of Charlotte and the United States Government—which is to say, by collective will of United States citizens—a huge robbery took place in Brooklyn, and the spoils are being divided. In economic terms, this is known as the "redistribution of wealth." But, when capital is flowing upwards, that description is not used. And now, yet another "strange and bitter crop"[11] grows from unredeemed soil.

9. Holiday, *Lady Sings the Blues*, 95.
10. "Latinx" is a gender-neutral term used rather than Latino/Latina.
11. Allan, "Strange Fruit." Used by permission.

The story of Brooklyn would be difficult enough if it stopped there, with just that one place. While the neighborhood was being razed by the collective action of city, state, and federal government, many residents and institutions there were encouraged to move west, just across the new highways being built, into the west side of Charlotte. This area is home to other historic African-American institutions and neighborhoods, including Johnson C. Smith University, a historically Black school, and the Washington Heights neighborhood, which during the day of streetcars was one of the only majority Black streetcar suburbs in the country. At that time, a significant and stable population of white people lived on the west side as well, in segregated neighborhoods where the dividing lines were often just streets that residents dared not cross.[12] But with the advent of the expressways and an influx of Black residents, leaving town to live in new suburbs while maintaining easy access to the economic center of the city became an attractive option for white folks.

Most white families who lived in West Charlotte during and right after urban renewal chose to leave. Massive demographic change happened quickly. The practice of "blockbusting" began in Charlotte at this time. Blockbusters were opportunistic investors who used fear of Black residents to coerce white families into selling their homes and land cheaply and quickly. Stable white families wanted out, for economic reasons that were understandable. Given the way that housing equity was built for white people through racial codes, the last families to leave would see the wealth they were trying to build through homeownership destroyed by a system that systematized the fear and hatred of Black people. Leaving was an act of protecting an investment. Soon enough, the dispossessed poured into the west side, looking for new homes in the aftermath of the violent destruction of their neighborhoods. The blockbusters were now landlords with huge holdings. They bought cheap but kept the prices high, which resulted in overcrowding. Families squeezed into small, overcrowded spaces to make their money stretch as far as possible.

The trauma of sudden land loss, of the plunder of wealth and the rending of the social fabric that stabilized neighborhoods for decades, cannot be underestimated. Author Mindy Fullilove calls it "root shock,"[13] as when a plant is uprooted from its soil, and thus loses its ability to thrive. For people

12. Among these people were Helms's paternal grandparents. Her father was born in the Smallwood neighborhood, just a mile from where we live today.

13. Fullilove, *Root Shock*.

of color in Charlotte, and across the United States, this episode of "root shock" that followed urban renewal echoed the historical traumas visited upon their communities for generations. The practice of forced displacement, where the ambition of a white power structure removes people from land, and land from people,[14] is repeated over and over in the history of European settlers and colonizers. From colonial expeditions to the Trail of Tears, the doctrine of discovery to urban renewal, displacement continues today. The next wave of urban displacement is gentrification. After making their homes in west side neighborhoods that have received very little city investment for forty years, Black residents are now in the path of plans being made by real estate developers, and enabled by municipal officials, without their input or consent. The renewed interest in the west side has coincided with new city investment in the area. Sidewalks, trees, greenways, traffic circles, and new businesses are all on the way, just in time for long-term residents not to be able to enjoy them.

The story of the displacement of common folks in the service of powerful economic interests is not new. The book of First Kings tells the story of Naboth, an Israelite who owns an ancestral vineyard. His property catches the eye of a house flipper who wants to purchase the vineyard to use for his own purposes. The house flipper wants to come in and make some quick changes by replacing generations of effort in cultivating a vineyard—slow, patient labor—with the quick work of planting a vegetable garden. The grapes, with their complex flavors developed over years, will be replaced with annual producers like summer squash and butterbeans. Naboth is not interested in making a deal. He recognizes that even if he accepts some cash for his vineyard, losing his connection to the soil and to the generations the preceded him on that soil will not be worth any amount of money. Connection between people, God, and land forms the basis of the Israelites' self-understanding. Selling the land violates God's law, Naboth claims. The trading of an ancestral place for a cash payout replaces the gift of generations with a temporary fix. Such a transaction fundamentally misunderstands the relationship between God, people, and land. Naboth refuses to participate.

Naboth has come up against a powerful force. The person making the cash offer for his place is King Ahab of Israel. Municipal reinvestment is happening in Naboth's area, and Ahab's sights are set on Naboth's

---

14. My friend the Rev. Dr. Rodney Sadler often says that "racism removes people from land and land from people." I learned to state the matter that way from him.

neighborhood. Ahab is used to getting what Ahab wants. So he calls in code enforcement, in the person of his wife Jezebel, to apply some pressure on Naboth. Ahab wants what he wants, and he is willing to do what he needs to get it. He knows that Jezebel plays for keeps, and that she can be used to sweeten the proposal to Naboth.

But Jezebel goes even further than just opportunistic sales tactics. She does not bother with mailing postcards offering cash for vineyards, or putting tacky signs reading "We Buy Vineyards For Cash" up and down his street. She decides to use the power of the courts to root Naboth out of his land. Shortly, Naboth is accused of idolatry. He is incarcerated, and then taken outside the city and stoned to death. And so Ahab takes possession of what he wanted all along. With unchecked power, and limitless appetite, Ahab is able to do what he wants in regards to Naboth's land. The relationships of Naboth to the soil, or of Naboth to his neighbors, or of Naboth to God as mediated through his ancestral place, cannot be spared once the mighty king sets his eyes on that valuable land. Kings and governments want what they want, and will build what they will build. The costs will be borne by other people, in bodies and in broken relationships and in root shock, as gardens of flourishing are destroyed to make way for new development.[15]

↭

There are big changes coming to Enderly Park. Neighbors sense that these changes are not for their benefit. Even for those who are able to manage the higher rents and real estate taxes, the new businesses, the upfitted gathering spaces, and the renovated blocks will not be for them. They will be for someone else, someone richer, someone with less melanin. These sorts of changes are often called "gentrification." I am really tired of talking about gentrification. This subject is in constant discussion around me, and yet talking about it never makes a change in the problem. So, I am attempting to eliminate the word from my vocabulary.

There are good reasons to stop talking about gentrification. For one, it obscures the roots of the problem it attempts to describe. By the time the kind of changes labelled as gentrification become visible, the damage is already done. The origin of that damage is in the way United States culture conceives of land ownership and development. Coffee shops and breweries,

15. You can find this story in 1 Kings 21. It goes pretty much the way I told it.

bike lanes and funky house renovations are signs of gentrification. But they are late signs. They are signs not of something starting, but of damage that has long been done. The outward signs happen only after decades of disinvestment, after governmental subsidies are consistently awarded to other parts of town, after lots of papers have been filed at the courthouse and many deeds have changed hands. Those processes are silent. They almost never involve the people whose homes and neighborhoods they will radically affect. By the time the first hipster bar shows up, the stage has been set and there is no turning back. Blaming the guy with the flannel shirt and waxed mustache or the lady with the jogging stroller can be cathartic—and indeed, they need to be attentive to how to be good neighbors in a new context—but it does not get at the roots of the issue.

Maybe the most compelling reason to eliminate the word "gentrification" from my vocabulary is that describing the shifts taking place in urban neighborhoods around the country as "gentrification" places the newcomers—the re-investors, the "urban pioneers," the gentry—at the center of the story. The terms of the discussion place the poor and people of color on the margins from the beginning. Without a different conversation—one that fully accounts for the roots of the problem, and the people harmed by the problem—the results will continue to be the same.

So, it is important to stop talking about gentrification. Instead, the story of urban change happening around the country at the beginning of the twenty-first century can be framed as *land loss* and *serial displacement*. Such a shift places the lives of people of color, who have long suffered from choices made to displace them and remove them from their land, front and center in the discussion. Changing the terms of the conversation helps to amplify the voices of the marginalized, who often go unheard in such discussions. When they are not heard, it is not for their lack of speaking or inability to understand what is happening. It is because some people choose not to listen.

These terms of conversation bring about a different way of looking at the problem, one that illuminates the history that preceded it and makes plain the cost of continuing to enact that history. By *land loss*, I mean simply that in neighborhoods around the country, including in Enderly Park, the poor are losing access to valuable land in ways that turn land into a commodity for trading, and the people who occupy it into numbers on spreadsheets. The U.S. economic system makes land ownership a primary means of building wealth. Those who own land are lifted up as achieving at least a portion of the so-called "American Dream." But even a cursory knowledge of U.S. history makes it clear that the opportunity to own land has been restricted in a variety of ways that have stripped people of color from land-owning and wealth-building opportunities while at the same time promoting and subsidizing that same opportunity for whites. The outcomes of that oppressive history are all around.

One of the ways that laws and policies keep housing and land-use inequities in place is by the design of landlord-tenant relationships. In North Carolina, tenant protections are very weak. The law almost always favors landlords, especially as it regards changes in land use and rental rates. When Jimmy's landlord decides that the lot he owns can be redeveloped to turn more profit, it will not matter for one second that Jimmy has lived there for seventeen years, that he has been the finest neighbor one could hope for, or that he has cared for the people and places of Enderly Park in quiet and meaningful ways far beyond what any of us neighbors have deserved. Jimmy will lose access to his land and his home. Development agencies will call that loss "progress" and roll out the red carpet for the developer who rebuilds on the plot he occupied. The municipal authorities will call it "revitalization," but Jimmy is very much alive. His vital signs are quite good.

To further complicate the problem, the North Carolina General Assembly has effectively outlawed cities and towns from setting their own regulations about the availability of affordable housing in their municipalities. The development lobby, fearing lower profit margins, has worked to help lawmakers craft policy that discourages or restricts mandatory inclusionary zoning policies, which could ensure the availability of workforce housing across our city. They have done this despite clear evidence that these policies are working in other places around the country. In other words, not only will Jimmy lose his place now, but the more affordable housing is torn down, the less clear it is that there will be sufficient housing for Jimmy's family in the future.

By *serial displacement* I mean that the injustice of land loss happens to the same marginalized groups, namely the poor and people of color, each time the changing whims of the market send land speculators to circle a new area. In the 1960s, the city of Charlotte razed the storied Brooklyn neighborhood, with its almost exclusively Black population, encouraging residents and institutions to migrate to West Charlotte. Fifty years later, guess which part of town thought leaders, planners, nonprofit groups, business boosters, and civic leaders can't stop dreaming about?

West Charlotte neighbors like Jimmy have taught me that there is no need for fancy words to describe what is happening.

"You can feel it," Jimmy told me.

"It is a punch in the gut, and you can't get your breath back," Michelle said.

They would know. Their people have known land loss and serial displacement from the time they were kidnapped and brought to this continent. In each chapter of history since then, the same themes emerge. And here it is in the air now, again. It constricts the throat, leaving folks gasping for air.

Curtis and I were riding home from church one day when I brought up the changes that are coming to Enderly Park. The new development had not reached Tuckaseegee yet, but it was on the edge of the neighborhood. I knew he had seen it, and I was curious what he thought. "Have you noticed those huge houses they are building just across the tracks from us?" I asked. What do you make of that?"

He had noticed, of course. The houses were built with the intention of being noticed. At 4,000 square feet, they dwarf the 1,000 square feet mill houses they are built next to. Curtis noticed, and he knew exactly what the new architecture meant.

"Everybody now is talking about moving back to the city," he said. "So what they are going to do is to push us out to the suburbs and they will come back to Tuckaseegee, and all the other neighborhoods close by and buy up all the property. That's the thing to do now if you have money. So we're just going to get pushed out. The rent will go up and we'll be headed out about 15 more bus stops to the other side of the highway."

Curtis knows intuitively what is coming. He knows that it won't be long before he has to start apartment hunting. The renovations and the tear-downs that will triple the size of the old mill houses here will all be signs that he is no longer welcome in the place he has called home for more than a decade. Curtis will not get a say in the matter when it happens. He knows within his body, whether he has words for it or not, that when white folks decide they want to take Enderly Park, they will do it regardless of what that means for the Black folks who live here.

Curtis's description of what is coming is summed up in his pronouns. There is a "them" and an "us." And those two categories break down along the usual lines. The poor and the middle class. People of color and white folks. The underclass and the propertied class. Many of those who will move here will cite the desire to be part of "a diverse neighborhood." But they are acting within an economic system built in such a way that diversity is always temporary. (During our Freedom Ride journey with the youth in 2015, we had breakfast with civil rights activist Dr. John Perkins in Jackson, Mississippi. He told us, "integration names the time between when the first white family moves in and the last Black family leaves.")

I fear that although my intentions are different, the results of my presence here will finally be the same. I have worked daily to build the kind of solidarity that has made me a part of the life of the neighborhood. I feel like one of "us." But I cannot be—I bear all the markers of being one of "them." The economic and political system that controls the fate of Enderly Park works by moving people around under the guise of "creating value." Serial displacement has roped me into the side of the displacers, whether I want to be there or not. My housing is not in jeopardy. In fact, I will have a nice payday coming if I decide to sell. The new amenities being built will be aimed at people who look like me and my children. The real-estate agents driving clients around will not stop to ask me about my intentions, or how I feel about the coming changes in the neighborhood. But the white families the agents drive around will find that seeing me walking on the sidewalk calms their nerves and increases the likelihood of their moving here.

Enderly Park is beginning to show outward signs of change by 2016, and so one night Helms and I walk down the street with our boys because the gentrifiers have invited us to supper. They would like a chance to get to know us and to learn about Enderly Park. I am immediately suspicious, and am determined not to provide them with any easy comfort about their decision to move here. Surely they are nice people, but even nice people act in systems that do terrible things. Things like the forced displacement of entire neighborhoods.

Walking into the yard—the biggest yard on Tuck—I feel the resistance in my body. My legs don't want to go this way, across the neat lawn and under the sprawling magnolia. I would be more comfortable at the corner store next door, or at the bus stop across the street. They welcome us on the porch, our kids hiding from theirs at first, and then dashing together behind the tall wooden fence around the back. I am still resisting, even as we shake hands, though I try to hide it. They must feel it too, the tension in my arm, the spirit of discomfort. As I enter the house, every fiber in my body screams that I don't want to be in this space.

They have picture molding, and they actually hang pictures from it. The shiny countertops, the antique replica door hardware, and the perfect hardwoods all speak to the level of care this house received that the neighborhood itself never got. I have seen the damage of disinvestment too closely to be comfortable in a place that provides meticulous renovation for only a select few.

Our kids do not have the same reservations Helms and I do. They play out of sight, and only re-appear when supper is ready. They eat quickly and then they scatter once more. I silently wonder what this means.

I try to settle in, feeling in some sense that I am betraying my neighbors by entering into this space. Appetizers and cold beer help me acclimate myself, as does pretending that this is a museum and not a house. The dinner is delightful—simple, with good conversation, which is frank and uncomfortable at times. We talk about what the presence of well-to-do white families entering the neighborhood means, about the lessons we have learned and about our discomfort in the situation. All of this is received openly. I start to recline at the table, my posture softening as it would at the beginning of a friendship. We are all laughing, I notice.

On the walk home, I begin to contemplate those feelings within my body. I move gently, with soft knees, as we walk the two blocks to the house. With my resistance lowered, I see a fear that I have to begin examining. What if my aversion to supper with the gentrifiers is because I see myself in them? In some ways, this is too painful to contemplate. I can see the damage coming. People I love are losing their homes, their community, their stability. They are losing me, and I am losing them. I am fighting it through activism, through helping to organize a community land trust, and by telling anyone who will listen. Though the odds seem long, Enderly Park might win the battle against unjust development practices and historical disinvestment.

But Enderly Park as it currently exists may not win the battle, and if not, I will be in a position to make a big profit, whether I want it or not. I cannot avoid that I bear all of the outward symbols of a gentrifier in my lack of melanin and my tow-headed children, my manner of dress and the way I keep my yard. This is the obvious part, which I know already. The painful step comes next. If all of the outward signs of my life show that my place in Enderly Park may be damaging to my neighbors, then I must ask, what is in the ground of my own soul? Whatever spiritual deficiency produces the fruit of serial displacement lives in me also. I cannot just cover that up. I need to root it out, no matter how costly. I see myself reflected in the mirror of the gentrifiers, and thus cannot avoid the question of how the habits of whiteness, of injustice, of the "white savior" complex have buried down within me in ways that I have not learned to notice yet. My body resists being in that house because my mind is not ready for the pain of seeing myself reflected there.

Yet though my body and mind resist seeing myself as a part of that space, as part of a system of displacement now affecting Enderly Park, as part of a people who have been displacers for as long as we have settled places on this side of the Atlantic, learning to see myself in this way is precisely the work I need to do. My resistance only serves me, not my neighbors, and it only serves me on the surface. Below the surface, it robs the nutrients from the soil of my soul. I come from a culture—white culture—that "does not know and does not want to know"[16] the harm we have done to ourselves, to our neighbors, and to the creation that sustains us by refusing to see the truth about ourselves. My unease in the home of the gentrifiers is shallow—it can be calmed by baby carrots and pale ale—because I have not dug deep enough yet. The excavation of my place, and my soul, and my soul's place in the world must go deeper.

At this moment in history, with rampant displacement sweeping through cities, and with the rise of white nationalism again trying to make the narrative of displacement and domination normal and acceptable, digging deeper into my soul is essential work for me to do. It is the work for all of us who think we are white to do. The fruit of the Spirit that enables us to do that excavation is love. Writing of love, Paul says that now, with partial, incomplete love, we see in a mirror, dimly.[17] Which is to say, not deeply enough. Not into the heart of things, the deep downness of ourselves. But then—when our love is perfect—we will see completely. We will see ourselves completely, will know ourselves fully, as we have been fully known. Souls that have excavated the weight of history, the many stories that our bodies hold, will no longer abide the suffering of our neighbors, for it will be our suffering. We will no longer rip them from their land, for we will be ripping them from ourselves. And we will finally be reconciled, to the soil

---

16. Baldwin, *The Fire Next Time*, 5.

17. 1 Corinthians 13:12.

that nurtures us, to our own souls, to our neighbors, and to the God who made us all.

One afternoon in late 2017, I walk into a local shop. By this time, rent has been going up for nearly a year, and the obvious signs of displacement are beginning to appear—houses with purple doors, a new neighborhood Facebook page, the presence of white people. A neighbor is one of the employees behind the counter. She is a lifelong resident, born on Tuck, who moved away for only a few years before returning. Her people were part of building the neighborhood, back when it was white and upwardly mobile. Back then, opportunity was not scarce. She had plenty of opportunity, but chose to come back and to stay through the lean times. I admire this greatly, but I also suspect she has stayed out of stubbornness rather than solidarity.

As I make my selection and approach the counter, she starts talking, but quietly. She cannot wait to bring up the economic and demographic changes that are coming our way. She wants me to know exactly how she feels about them.

"You know, a lot of things are changing here right now," she says. "The rents are going up and things are getting better. And I am excited."

She needs no prompt to start this. She keeps her voice low, though. There are other customers in the room making their selections.

"I know," I respond. "Things are changing, and I agree that some are exciting. But you know, I worry about what that means for the people that live here now. I wonder how we can help keep them here if they want to stay."

"Oh, I don't worry about that. I want them out of here. Gone, across the highway," she points westward. "I want it to go back to the way it used to be. I want it to go up, up, up, up, up, up, up."

Seven "ups." I counted.

She sounds like she is expecting me to push back, so I take a different approach. "What was it like back then?" I ask. I know what she is saying— "how it used to be"—but I want her to say it.

She thinks for a second. How can she say what she is thinking without saying what she is thinking?

"Safe."

Pause.

"No thugs."

Pause.

"Beautiful."

I let it sit for a moment. We both hear the echo in the shop, and we both see other customers moving towards the register. There are only a couple of moments left in this encounter.

She means "white." And I see it in her face that now she is embarrassed. She knows that I know, and she is embarrassed that I know, and she is a little embarrassed that she thought it, and especially that she almost made the subtext into text.

She wants to make the neighborhood white again. She thinks that will make it great again. She hears the echo, and squirms a bit while it keeps bouncing around the room, keeps repeating in both of our heads.

"I worked hard for what I have, you know," she says.

Ah, "hard work." The refuge of the willfully ignorant. I did not ask about that. Did not wonder. So I just let it sit again, the echo still bouncing around while I try to grab the right words. They ought to come more easily, but I am a little surprised at where this encounter has gone. I am tempted to turn over tables of this money exchange, and at the same time wondering how to keep the conversation open so I can convert her at a later time. When she is ready to meet Jesus, I could even baptize her in Stewart Creek, which runs down at the bottom of Parkway Avenue and through—this is almost too good to be true—Martin Luther King, Jr. Park.

Coming to grips with what she thinks, maybe for the first time, she says "Well, I guess I do worry a little about the poor people. But I still want things to go up, up, up."

"So do I," I respond. "I want things to go up, but people of color and poor folks always get the short end of the stick when neighborhoods start changing. I don't see why they can't be here to get some of the profit. I think you and I ought to work on that."

And at that, a line is forming, cutting us off before we can wade in further. Before we can state the unstated. She calls the next customer up. The conversation is over for now, but it will keep echoing in my head, and up and down Tuckaseegee, for a long time yet.

Around the same time, Carolyn appears at the back door. She is the kind of neighbor we welcome to the back door. She loves to slip into the garden, admiring the flowers and salivating over the green tomatoes. She likes the tomatoes just OK when they are red, but she loves frying them green. I do not understand this. There are few sensual pleasures that rival a tomato sandwich. I spend most of the year waiting for the first ripe to-matoes to appear in my garden in June. From there on, every day through August brings the opportunity for two slices of bread, a slather of mayo, a dash of pepper, and a couple of slices of fresh tomato.

I know that a good Christian is not supposed to count the cost of our sacrificial gifts to the world. Christians believe in abundance, and not scar-city, and all that. But when Carolyn asks for some of those green tomatoes, and she always does, it hurts me. I say yes, usually, but when we walk out to the garden to pick them, the path between the mural and the strawberry plants is a tortured walk. Every step takes us closer to robbing the tomatoes of their potential.

On the afternoon she comes to the back door, Carolyn is worried. She is always worried, actually, but today it is more acute. A couple of days prior, the couple on the other side of her duplex got a letter in the mail from a new property management company. The letter told them that they had 30 days to vacate the property. The owner has decided "to go in a different direction," it reads, which is a not-so-subtle way of saying that they are not welcome as tenants anymore. Carolyn suspects that, as the resident on the other side of the duplex, she will receive a letter confirming the termination of her lease soon. She has come by on this day to talk about it. Unfortu-nately, there is not much we can do, at least nothing that will do anything but delay the inevitable. We agree to hold out hope for her for now, and to do what we can to help her neighbors find a place nearby. Neither of us can imagine Enderly Park without Carolyn or her neighbors.

After the shock wears off for Carolyn's neighbors, one of them calls the management company. He volunteers to do the needed repair work for free. There is a good bit of deferred maintenance that the landlord has been putting off, but as the tenant, he is willing to do it at his own expense if the landlord will allow him to stay. He has tinkered in the past to keep things livable, but now is willing to be more thorough about it if that will help him stay in place. This will cost him above and beyond the rent, but it will save his home.

"Sir," the property manager says, "your landlord is not interested in housing anymore. The land that the house is on is becoming very valu-able, and he only wants to capitalize on the value of the land, not to make improvements on the house."

The call makes plain the cruel future barrelling Carolyn's way. She will be leaving, probably soon. The afternoon visit is to let me know that. Her anxiety grows as we talk.

"I don't know where I will go," she says. "I don't have any place to go. And since I got laid off recently, I don't have any money. I don't know what I'm gonna do." The weight of this hangs between us in the humid air. I don't know what she will do either. And I know that this conversation will be repeated many times over in the coming months, with many other people.

The silence lingers for a few moments. Both of us know where this leads, and that we can do nothing to stop it. Neither of us is ready to name that yet.

"Brother Greg, do you have any green tomatoes in the garden yet?"

I hand her a basket. "Pick it clean, Sister Carolyn."

Here is "a strange and bitter crop"[18]—to nourish soil, to live through droughts and hailstorms and whirlwinds, to dig deep roots, and despite all the odds, to see the fruits slowly forming and moving toward ripeness. And then, to be told by people you have never seen that you will not eat of the fruits nourished by your resilience, watered by your sweat and tears.

18. Allan, "Strange Fruit."

8

Epistrophy[1]

I IMAGINE A CHIMNEY swift's daily agenda is simple. Morning exercise. Ruin some worm's afternoon plans. Eat blackberries. Plant and fertilize blackberry seeds. Tweet. Soar. Ride a warm breeze above the treeline, looking down at the way the creek seeks out the bottoms of the hills.

The little swift's evening is reserved for ritual. On a cloudless evening, the dusk sky becomes a movie screen. In the backyard theater, Helms and I and the boys lie still—as still as little boys can—while the light dims. On the blue-gray screen, fist-sized birds begin to swirl in response to an ancient call. We call them the "circle birds" because they fly circles around the church, gathering themselves in from east and west, from near and far. Circling, circling, they turn round and round and round the building. With ten minutes until sunset, several hundred black darts bob and weave across the screen. Something in the earth calls them home, to the corner of Tuckaseegee and Parkway, for two weeks each September. For years, even while no person used the church building, they have kept vigil here in late summer. A flock of chimney swifts returns to the same chimney each year. Enderly Park has been a part of this ancient ritual for longer than anyone here can remember.

They keep turning round the building. The older ones chirp in delight to be together again. Every minute or so, some unknown cue tells them to change paths. A few break off. The rest follow, scattering the circle that was moving clockwise around the chimney. In only a few seconds, the circle

---

1. Monk, "Epistrophy."

birds are again in unison, now counterclockwise, turning round once more while the light lasts.

Their arc is wide. From it, they see Carolyn's house, the one where she lives for now, but probably not for much longer. They glide over the high-dollar renovations at the former trap house. Turning, turning, they sail over the spot where Keith breathed his last. The circle tightens as daylight fades and the call home crescendos. Now from the garden we watch them circle the old willow oak on the corner, the one that has been watching this show for longer than anyone. They circle that corner, that sacred corner, the corner where it happened—where grief flowed like rivers and sadness like a mighty stream. And the birds, with an ancient call in their bones, swirl around us, drawing us into their vortex as we lie dizzy in the garden.

The sun settles quickly, just before eight, on a mid-September evening. The air is still thick with summer, but the birds ride a breeze that holds the first hints of autumn. And as they turn around and around the church, the waning light reminds them to head to roost. One by one, as the North Star begins to peek out of the heavens, birds leave the circle and dive into the chimney. The screen behind them grows a deeper gray as the flock thins, until finally only a few black darts bob in and out of the picture. Teenagers, surely. Pushing the limits. But after a few minutes, the sky is still, as the last one dives down into its home to rest, for tomorrow they will turn round and round again. Tomorrow they will eat and sing and fly and struggle, and then will turn round and round again.

With the sky quiet, Helms and I take the boys in for their nighttime ritual. Brushing teeth. Singing songs. Reading books. More songs. And then, just as the house is settling down, just as our minds are quieting down—KNOCKKNOCK. KNOCKKNOCK.

Victor walks in. In the manner of family, he makes a quick knock and bursts right through the door. I enjoy this most of the time. Only most of the time. Sometimes the constant series of knocks on the door can be exhausting, so that by the time the sun finally sets, I hope that the door stays closed for good. Which rarely happens. On a few stressful days, I have considered nailing it shut. But the neighborhood is changing now, and the sorts of friendships that burst through the door without warning are becoming more and more rare. The people who practice that kind of neighborliness are being forced out.

On this night, Victor is a bit more lively than is typical, and he is already quite an energetic character. His day off has been used for having a good time, and that has included a bit of strong beverage. He is not drunk, but he is part ways there. He is at that stage of inebriation where, with inhibitions lowered, real feelings that normally stay concealed can come out.

Victor has come to tell me that he loves me. That is the only purpose of his visit. Even with a couple of beers in him, it takes him a minute to get to it. He takes the circuitous route. He circles around what he wants to say, hinting at what is coming.

"You know, I was thinking about you tonight. I just want to tell you that, well, I mean, we've taken a lot of trips together. To the beach. To the mountains. Camping. To your parents' house." He is circling.

"And I was thinking, we've had some arguments in the past, but you know, well. . ." He keeps turning around it.

"I mean, we've had some good times, too. Laughing, acting crazy, going swimming. . ." Still circling.

"You helped me to be a better person. I got baptized because of y'all, and now I'm going to church, and loving God, and reading my Bible every day."

I wonder if he will get to the point. Talking religion is usually a way to keep people at a distance. Jesus-talk recruits someone who is not in the room into the mess. Jesus isn't there to speak up for himself, so he gets used to relieve the anxiety that comes with talking about love or anger, things that matter. But Victor is not using that strategy. The Spirit is moving in this moment, perhaps aided by some spirits, but still, the Spirit is alive and present.

Finally, he spits it out. "I just want you to know I love you." He listens to the sound of it for a second before he goes on. "And if someone ever did something to you, you wouldn't even have to call me. I would know, and I would come right up here and cut a fool," he says. That is street talk for "I've got your back."

"And if someone messes with those boys of yours, I will cut a damn fool."

This is what love looks like. It is the knowledge that when you need it, somebody's got you. The way that our lives have been stitched together—a laugh here, a minor conflict there, a couple visits in jail and another in the hospital, an evening around the table, a deep truth spoken in a tense moment—means that in trouble, we know that we have one another's backs.

We know where to turn in the future because we both know where we have turned in the past. One particular night, not too long after our little religious community moved into Enderly Park, I walk down into the partial basement of our house to grab a tool, only to be greeted by a horrific smell. Something has gone seriously wrong. After a little exploring with a housemate, we figure out what it is—a series of problems have led to a huge backup in our plumbing. And though we cannot understand how, one of the clean-off caps on the main exit pipe has come off. We've been flushing the toilet directly in the basement for weeks. Maybe months. Shit.

We are broke, and we are short on tools and possibly good sense as well. So the plan is for the housemate and I to start hauling buckets of the current contents of our basement as far from any houses as we can carry it. And then, we will improvise some tools to dig out the problematic contents of the pipe. This, we hope, will at least create a short-term solution until we can find money for full plumbing surgery.

Sometimes when Victor walks into the house unannounced, he is right on time. This particular night, I have never been so happy to see him. And he is the kind of guy who, when I tell him what is happening, immediately walks home, grabs his work boots, and starts helping out. There is nothing you can do to deserve that sort of friendship. When you find a friend who will get in your excrement up to his elbows, you have found a gift you can never be worthy of.

We work together for hours to make things manageable. Emptying our basement-turned-cesspool is as awful as it sounds, but we laugh our way through it. And when things are flowing again, we shower. Then we shower again. And then we celebrate at an all-night diner.

After more than a few hard times in community and as a neighbor in Enderly Park, stories like this give me hope. I smile when I think of the way we worked together, and of how I have been so deeply loved that working with me to excavate my basement of my you-know-what was not even a question for Victor. It was an automatic response. When other tough times come, the memory of working together in such a way still lives in our bodies, even after the stench has left our noses. Trials return, but we have a well to draw on that calls us back to our truest selves. A deep truth about the possibility of human flourishing exists within that basement. We can dig our way out of the messes we live in by the sort of love that grabs a shovel and a bucket and lays down its life for its friends.

I want Victor to know—and I want to be able to say—that I love him as well. So on the night he comes in to tell me he loves me, I meet his gaze while he says it. He looks right into my eyes, and I look into his. We hold that for a lengthy period, not letting go. These moments are too rare. This gift is too precious. We know, and we are known, if not in fullness, then still at a deeper level than we can describe with words. But we have a story for it. We remind each other of that night in the basement sometimes. It is our way of renewing our vows.

A sacred moment is here. I usually do not know when such a moment arrives. I only figure it out later. But this evening, with Victor, I know what is happening. And so I want Victor to know that I love him. I want Victor to know that I know that he loves me. I want these things because right in my living room—what an unexplainable gift has arrived!—is the kind of love that turns people around. Both of us know that love has turned each of us around. When dozens of the saints gathered several years prior to join Victor around the waters of baptism, it was because love turned him around. When Victor helped me to begin seeing through the lies of race by proclaiming that I am not a white man, and then offering me some new ways forward, love was turning me around.

In the Hebrew Bible, the term used for the theological idea of "conversion" is a word that means "to turn around." The image of this language is of a person walking in the wrong direction, then stopping and moving in the other direction. To be converted is to change paths. To experience a conversion is to have your eyes and your body fixed on one goal, but while you are moving toward that goal, you get stopped. Your aim gets changed. Your new direction points you to another destination. Maybe even to a whole new way of being.

No one manages to turn around alone. Moving in a different direction requires someone to help you see a different way. It takes at least one neighbor who loves you. Probably more than one, and probably over a long time. Victor is a great example of this, but he is certainly not the only one who has offered me the spacious hospitality that has allowed me to move in a different direction. When I walked into Shawn and Jake's room at summer camp, I thought one thing about myself and my relationship with those young men. When I turned around to leave, I was beginning to reflect on how that relationship needed to change, and what I needed to learn from that encounter. In the same way, carrying youth across the South turned me around again, drawing me closer into solidarity with them. And Charles Jones offered other moments of turning around, reminding me that the path I am attempting to walk has been blazed by generations of elders whose work has made mine possible. Every sacred moment that arrives is yet another opportunity to turn around once more, to circle back around towards home with a flock of friends on a sacred corner.

⌐φ

Thelonious Monk sometimes got up from the piano in the middle of a song to dance. One recurring dance of his, while squeezed between keyboard and piano bench in some tiny New York City club, was just turning in a circle. The sizzle of the hi-hat might get into him, or the thrum of the bass. Playing the piano became secondary to answering the call sounding in his feet and hips. The few surviving videos of this spontaneous dance do not show him to be a great dancer. Such concerns are secondary when the band is really swinging, though.

Monk, born in Rocky Mount, North Carolina, in 1917, was a bit of an eccentric. He sometimes got up from the piano not to dance, but perhaps to visit the bar, or go for a walk. When the music within him spoke, he listened. And listening, he became one of the most original voices in jazz music. Monk is remembered not so much for his unusual character, but for his unique compositions and his unconventional playing. The music he offered the world surprised and delighted. It challenged, and it journeyed to unexpected places. Monk could make the wrong notes sound right. And he could make the piano do things that pianos don't do. Once, at a 1963 demonstration with his friend, the Julliard professor Hall Overton, Monk showed his unusual technique for "bending" a note on the piano, resulting in a sound like a guitar player bending a string. After Monk's demonstration, Overton said, "That can't be done on piano, but you just heard it."[2]

Among Monk's early, and best-known, compositions is "Epistrophy," co-written with the drummer Kenny Clarke in 1941. The tune became one of the the essential compositions within the jazz literature. Students still study it today, and performers still play it.

In literature, epistrophe describes the repetition of a word or phrase at the end of consecutive lines or sentences.[3] In the "Love Chapter," Paul

2. Stephenson, "Is This Home?"

3. Edwards, *Epistrophies*, 1–26. I am grateful for the brilliant work of Brent Hayes Edwards. This recent book helped to inspire the theme and organization of this chapter, and is a fascinating study in the way jazz musicians used words.

writes, "When I was a child, I spoke like a child, I thought like a child, I reasoned like a child."[4] The repetition of "child" makes this an epistrophe. Monk's tune is the musical conception of the same idea. A figure is stated in the first measure, then repeated in the second measure. Another figure, a variation on the first, is stated in the third measure, then repeated in the fourth measure. The tune consists almost entirely of the repetition of those two figures, moving through two different keys. As an epistrophe in literature gets in the ears, and ultimately the memory of the reader or listener, so does the tune "Epistrophy." After just one hearing, identifying the song is easy. It takes up residence in the memory.

Epistrophe demands listeners' attention. It is a crag to hang on to, a little foothold to cling to in the experience of a work of art. When words and ideas become overwhelming, epistrophe creates a landscape to circle around, a way to stay connected to a rush of new ideas or images. A repeated word or phrase becomes a place to stand. It makes a place for an accent to land.

Repetition invites rhythm. Rhythm suggests music, and so epistrophe makes plain the connection between words and music. This connection is always present, even when it is unnoticed. Words spoken have pitch and accent. Speakers speed up and slow down for emphasis. Speech rises and falls as bebop does, darting between ideas, linking them together, making new connections from the same limited palette of notes or letters. In the construction of an improviser's solo or a lover's soliloquy, repetition highlights the thing that really needs to be said, and plants it in the memory. It allows the listener to stop moving for a moment, and instead to hold an idea or phrase, to turn slowly around it, to grasp it and see what it reveals.

The term "epistrophe" comes from Greek. Translated to English, it means "turning around." In literature and in Monk, it is the repetition of one small bit of material that builds memory and orients the reader or listener to a key idea or movement. Turning around gets you disoriented to the place you currently are, and then reorients you to the new place you are headed. Monk's "Epistrophy" does this with nearly every measure. Melody, harmony, and rhythm work together to make the literary device musical. The experience of "Epistrophy" is an ongoing cycle of disorientation and reorientation. No sooner does the piece trek down one path than it is reoriented into another one, one that is still related, but yet different. As the old Shaker hymn says, this turning is delight, "'til by turning, turning we come

4. 1 Corinthians 13:11.

'round right." Or, as Count Basie exclaimed with joy while starting up the big band for another reprise through a coda, "One more once!"

To walk in the way of Jesus is a constant turning. It is a consistent pattern of disorientation and reorientation. I need to be unsettled and disoriented. Inhabiting the body and the thought-world of a white man, a part of my story is that my people have settled into other people's places and reoriented their worlds to us. Both directly and indirectly, my people have profited from the work and the suffering of people of color in the United States, some of whom were here before my people arrived, and some of whom were brought in bondage. I could, without trying too hard, live my entire life without ever being turned around. My privilege is that the world has to reorient itself to me and to people like me. Being turned around does not come naturally. My people are accustomed to turning the world in our direction.

So what does it look like to get converted—to be turned around—when you are a part of a culture that assumes the world turns around you? White folks have been fed the lie that we are normal, or typical, that we are the standard in everything, from beauty to intellect to culture to theology. We have been fed the lie so long that we believe it. We think we need it. We rely on it as we rely on the warmth of summer and the cool of winter. And as it comes undone, the loss of the lie feels like oppression. But it is freedom.

In Baldwin's letter to his nephew, he makes plain the ways that the system of white supremacy has been visited upon his namesake. James was born into a neighborhood in which it was "intended that [he] should perish." His ambition was to be "limited" because the society "spelled out with brutal clarity . . . that [he was] a worthless human being . . . who was expected to make peace with mediocrity."[5] The "details and symbols of your life have been deliberately constructed to make you believe what white people say about you," Baldwin tells him.[6]

Baldwin's statements to his nephew have another side. The other side of disadvantage is domination or privilege. Naming the ways that domination and privilege show up in my life is an essential aspect of the work that I need to do with my sons, with my nieces, with my family and friends. So, I am taking Baldwin's letter as a guide, and writing a similar letter to my sons as a way of encouraging and challenging them. The letter reads like this:

5. Baldwin, *The Fire Next Time*, 7.
6. Baldwin, *The Fire Next Time*, 8

Dear children,

I am writing to you because I love you. And as it is with people who love one another, I have to try to tell you some hard things, things that are difficult to understand and even harder to change. But we cannot be free until we change them, and we cannot change them until we understand them.

You know already from the history you have learned and the lives that you live that we live in a land where not everyone is treated equally. As white people, every aspect of our lives has been built to make us believe that we are superior.[7] Our people—people like us, people who are called "white"—were born into the places where we were born not because we deserved or merited those places, but because we are white and for no other reason. You may not feel this all of the time. You might never feel this. But history bears it out. We are expected to make peace with our terrible mediocrity, and at the same time to have it rewarded as excellence. Our ambition is to be without limits, as are our appetites, because we can claim anything we want as ours. We need little discipline, for we can go where we want and do what we want how we want without fear of having our bodies confiscated, and without being allowed to fall too far. Our society spells out with brutal clarity, and in every place we look, that we are superior human beings. You know this is not true, and I expect you, and us together, to live into something that is true.

Do you remember the trips we made to the state fair in the fall of each year? Among all the stuff to do there—the food, the rides, the animals—you and your mom sometimes went into the fun house. Along the path through the fun house, there were mirrors. One made you look like you had the legs of a giraffe. Another made you short and as wide as a hippopotamus. One made you look big and tall and wide, and it blurred everything else around you. The images in those mirrors are like how our culture works. Our culture, the culture of white people, distorts reality. It makes us see things differently than how they really are.

In America, the fun house mirror moves people around. It takes people like us and moves us to the center of the reflection, and moves people like our neighbors—people with more melanin in their skin—off to the edge. Sometimes it moves them out of the picture altogether. The mirror of

7. Baldwin, *The Fire Next Time*, 7–8. This sentence and the rest of the paragraph mimic closely the structure and grammar of the section of Baldwin cited, but in a way that addresses those of us who are given the unmerited privilege awarded to white folks in the system of white supremacy.

our culture makes us and our families look bigger and more important, and our neighbors and their families look smaller and less important.

You have already learned that this hurts our neighbors. We often talk about some of the ways it hurts them. Sometimes they lose their homes, or they do not have enough food, or their families have to live apart from each other because of unfair laws and unfair policing. You know this, and you see it, and you hate it already, and I love that about you. But I need to tell you that although you cannot see it yet, this culture is harming you, too. And me. And everybody who thinks they are white. When we see the reflection that places us at the center, it keeps us from seeing the truth about ourselves. It gives us a role in the story that does not belong to us, at least not all the time. There is a long history among our people of thinking we are heroes who bring good news and save the day. There may have been times when our people were heroes, but many times our people have been on the wrong side of stories. We have taken other people's land, or their children. Our people stole other people's futures. There are bad chapters in our story. We have to tell them also. We especially have to tell them, so that we can stop repeating them.

Though we try to love our neighbors, trying does not stop us from getting hurt by the mirrors that distort reality. In this place called the United States of America, we start to see funny. Our vision gets messed up. Even though we know it is wrong, we start to think that the fun house mirror is a real mirror. We start building neighborhoods of fun houses, which turns out to be no fun for anyone.

This is hard to understand, my children, and it keeps getting deeper. It begins to feel natural that the world works according to the rules of race, even though there is nothing natural about race. Neighborhoods are not naturally divided by race. People's ability to earn and save money and then pass it on to their kids is not naturally different because of the color of their skin. Mayors and governors and presidents are usually white, but this is not because our people are always best fit for the jobs. And we don't have superior hearts or pancreases, even though our neighbors have heart disease and diabetes more frequently than our families do.

All of these differences have come about because of decisions our ancestors made when they were building the United States and its culture. And those decisions have a cost. Choosing one thing requires leaving something else behind. Some of the costs of the cultural, and political, and economic, and theological decisions that our ancestors made along the lines of race are easy to see. You know already that our neighborhood is being torn apart by gentrification and the forced movement of people we love. You know some of the history of our city, that this is not the first time forced movement has happened. You don't know the fancy terms for it yet, but you know how unfair rules have been forced on our neighbors. You have seen the violence done by policy. Together, we are learning to name that violence—health disparities, lack of opportunity, the education gap, mass incarceration, the school-to-prison pipeline.

Learning to name those issues is important, my children, but learning only matters if it moves you to act. The first act is to turn around. To stop looking in the fun house mirror. To face the other way and to see the world as it really is, and to see our place in it, and to run towards freedom. I would like for us to run together.

But running towards freedom does not mean running away from our people. Once we get our eyes fixed, we will have to go back. You see, white folks have been using the fun house as home base. They even send out missionaries from there, and get other people to think those crazy mirrors are real. Together, we have to return to them, and to the mirrors of distortion, and preach some good news. That sounds easy, but our people love the distorted realities of the fun house. It will take a while to talk them out. And who knows, sometimes we might get drawn back in ourselves. But if we stick together, and pray together, and sing together, and listen to what we have heard our neighbors teaching us, we will start taking that fun house down piece by piece until it is no more. And when we finish, we will look out at the crowds of the carnival. And they will be so beautiful. My God, they are beautiful. And finally, we will get to be a part of them.

The work will be hard. It may be dangerous, for the demand of white folks above all else is that we keep the silence and maintain the lies of race. But we have lived too long near the ugly underside of those lies. We cannot be silent anymore. We will not be silent anymore. Besides, we come from a long line of malcontents and ne'er-do-wells from the rolling hills of the western piedmont of North Carolina. We owe it to them, and we owe it to ourselves—and maybe most importantly, we owe it to our neighbors—to finally rebel for the right reason.

Yours in Love,

Dad

There is a story in the Gospels where Jesus approached a man by a pool in Jerusalem. The pool was known for its healing qualities. When the water in the pool got stirred up, the infirm waiting near it would race to its waters in hopes of being healed. One man there had been ill for thirty-eight years. When Jesus approached him, holding within himself the power to heal, he asked him a most important question: "Do you want to be made well?"[8]

At the time I am writing this book, I am thirty-eight years old, and I want to be made well. To be made well means receiving the gifts of my neighbors, whose lives invite me into a life of thriving built on solidarity. It means learning to see the hidden wounds caused by systems of supremacy and domination, wounds that I bear though I cannot always see them. Tending to those wounds is part of the work of God's justice in the world. What happened to the souls of the men who ran the bulldozers that razed neighborhoods during urban renewal? How did they go to their homes at night when their jobs were to destroy other people's homes during the day? Or, what happens to the interior life of settlers, both colonial-era and modern, who claim that everything they see is theirs? What good is it to be on the beneficial side of health disparities if the extra years you live come at the cost of the vitality of your soul? And what does it mean to be part of a people who willingly forget that these stories are part of our heritage, and so keep repeating them? I have to keep digging for the answers to these questions.

Being made well, at this point in my life and at this point in history, means getting turned around. Turned to see my neighbors in the depth of their beauty and goodness, and to see brokenness—mine and theirs—truthfully. Turned around from the clownish fun house mirror into a true vision of where I have come from and where I am now, and where I might go, given the grace to move into the fullness of life.

Turning from my brokenness, woundedness even, means wrestling with the hidden wounds that live in me. Those wounds keep me from full communion with my neighbors and bind me to a self-conception based in domination and superiority rather than neighborliness. The work of justice is soul work. The grace of being turned around might help change the world. It will certainly change me. It will give me new songs to sing, and new ways to sing old songs.

8. John 5:6.

I wonder what the man in Jerusalem did there, near the pool, for thirty-eight years. Why not just move on? I wonder whether he was trying very hard. Perhaps he came to identify so closely with his wounds that he did not want to move quickly when the waters began to stir. Perhaps he was easily distracted, always engaged in a secondary task. Maybe he was facing another way, gazing towards that which could not give life. Looking the wrong way may be the deepest temptation. Idolatry is just that—gazing at something that cannot heal.

In the words of the prophet Isaiah, "healing springs up quickly"[9] for the people whose lives get oriented to God's justice in the world. For the ones who loose the bonds of injustice, who share their bread with the hungry, who turn their faces toward the needs of the oppressed and afflicted, healing is not far off. Those who get made well—who choose to accept the gift of healing and who do the work of justice—get counted in that number of the saints whose lives got turned around. For them, a little riff—the rustling of water, say, or maybe a neighbor who loves them—becomes the stuff for building thriving community.

⌒

I am driving Alicia home one night following our weekly youth group meeting. She is the young woman with the knack for words. Between neighborhood, church, and her being our favorite babysitter, Alicia spends a lot of time with my family. As we near her house, she begins to speak something on her heart. She, as at some point do all the great minds and hearts in the world, is thinking about luck and fate.

"I've been thinking about some of those kids we used to go to summer camp with," she says, thinking back to those weeks at Mars Hill College. "I see how their lives are different, and how they seem to have everything. But I seem to have all the bad luck. Stuff does not work out for me in the same way. Everything is a struggle, from getting to school, to having to move a lot, to dressing the right way and having the same stuff that they have, to planning for my future. It's just so unfair."

Alicia sees that the world is organized, and not in her favor. Opportunity is unavailable and fortune has conspired against her. She is on an interminable run of bad luck. It is not that her life is merely suffering and

9. Isaiah 58:8.

drudgery. She lives a life filled with love and joy and laughter, full of little acts of beautiful resistance that carve out spaces for flourishing. But she knows that her flourishing is won in spite of the dominant culture, not because of it. She knows "the struggle" intimately, and she is not afraid to talk about it.

Alicia also knows that there are some born with extraordinary luck. I am one of them. Privilege is no guarantee of success, but the landing place when you fall is not nearly so far down. Unearned merit gives the appearance of flourishing, but sometimes it is only a facade. Beneath it lies the knowledge that privilege has costs to everyone. It damages the neighborhoods, the families, and the bodies of those from whom it is withheld, while deadening the spirits of the privileged, building distance from neighbors and soil and soul.

Alicia is not afraid to name any of this, nor is she scared to state her feelings about it. She sees the way the bad luck piles up, how moving a little burden out of the way, for her, becomes mountaintop removal. She sees that life is not that way for everyone. And, she sees that privilege comes at a cost for the privileged as well. We talk about this regularly, and we help each other to think about it.

I have come to see that finding ways to unlearn as much of the dominant culture as possible, by getting into the streets of Enderly Park, has been the way that Jesus has been using to get me saved. I am a white Baptist preacher from the Bible Belt. My people and I are Babylon, willing to join with any number of Nebuchadnezzars, ancient and modern. When it comes to ransacking land, pillaging bodies, and exiling people, we long ago cast our lots with the Empire.

But the call of Jesus—Come out my people![10]—is not only for those oppressed by Nebuchadnezzar. It is also a call to freedom for the Babylonians, whose identity is built on a narrative of scarcity, who believe that neighbors are to be fenced out and regulated away. To be one of Nebuchadnezzar's people is to rest easy with the deck stacked in your favor, to look at a trail of tears from an exiled people and not to be able to see why their grief matters. Coming out of that empire—getting turned around to see God, neighbor, and land in the fullness of their beauty—is only done with fear and trembling, and by returning more than once to set free those whom Nebuchadnezzar seduced with his call.

10. Revelation 18:4.

The habits learned in Babylon do not die easily, nor does their death in one or two Babylonians break the system that creates exiles and destroys cities. And even with those who manage to break away and return home, as with Nehemiah, new systems of oppression show up. Nebuchadnezzar gets reborn. The battle to be free from his influence is ongoing. God is always calling God's people out, inviting them to improvise a new path toward freedom from inside the constraints of the empire.

The journey home, and the renewing of a flourishing Jerusalem, nearly kills the Jewish people. What might it be for a Babylonian who joins them? To leave home, and privilege, and a place where it is possible to access all of the powers of the Empire makes little of the world's sense. The benefits of being Nebuchadnezzar's people are real, and they persist. They do not go away. There are all sorts of habits that have to be unlearned, and ways of thinking that must be given up, and no one goes to such places without much tribulation. But you can always go back. The journey to freedom must be chosen each day. Only over a lifetime, and only with the extraordinary and undeserved kindness of those who have been oppressed, can one of Nebuchadnezzar's troops join forces with the displaced band of the exiled on that journey.

This journey will be hard, in other words. It may be impossible. Yet, I try on that ride home to express to Alicia why I think my change of fortunes—my turning around, away from Babylon and into the desert heat of an oppressed place—has been the greatest thing to happen in my life.

"Alicia, I agree with you. Everybody has luck, and it seems like some people seem to get all the bad luck, and others get all the good luck. But for me, I want you to know that I think my luck has changed, and you are part of the reason. I think that for me—a white guy, from a place of privilege, with a different culture—to get to share my life with you, and your family, and the neighbors in Enderly Park, is the best thing that has happened to me. I have received so much love. Far more than I could ever deserve. And I have learned to see and hear the whole world differently. It has turned me around. I'm so lucky that has happened."

"I know what you mean," she replies. "I see the way people look at me when I'm with you and Helms. When we are walking around on the street or in a store or something, they look at me and wonder why some random Black girl is with you, or why some random white people are with me. They don't get it, that all of us belong together."

All of us belong together. Which is a little riff for building a new world.

I pull into her driveway, bursting with gratitude. We exchange a fist bump, and she bounds into the night, ready to set the world on fire with love. I back out of her driveway to turn around again, having encountered a love that fills my heart with song. I am home, and it fills my heart with song.

Bibliography

"Alexander, Sydenham Benoni." *Biographical Dictionary of the United States Congress.* http://bioguide.congress.gov/scripts/biodisplay.pl?index=A000102.

Baldwin, James. "As Much Truth As One Can Bear." In *The Cross of Redemption: Uncollected Writings,* edited by Randall Kenan. New York: Vintage, 2010.

———. *The Fire Next Time.* New York: Vintage, 1993.

Balentine, Samuel E. *Prayer in the Hebrew Bible: The Drama of Divine-Human Dialogue.* Minneapolis: Fortress, 1993.

Baraka, Amiri. Liner notes for "Coltrane Live at Birdland." Impulse IMPD-198, 1996, compact disc.

Barber, William J., with Jonathan Wilson-Hartgrove. *The Third Reconstruction: How a Moral Movement is Overcoming the Politics of Division and Fear.* Boston: Beacon, 2016.

Berry, Wendell. *A Timbered Choir: The Sabbath Poems 1979–1997.* Washington, DC: Counterpoint, 1998.

Boschma, Janie, and Emily Deruy. "Where Children Rarely Escape Poverty." *The Atlantic,* March 7, 2016. https://www.theatlantic.com/education/archive/2016/03/poor-children-rarely-escape-poverty-here/472002/.

Brueggemann, Walter. *The Psalms and the Life of Faith.* Minneapolis: Augsburg Fortress, 1995.

Capwell, Jessica. "Youth group in Charlotte's Enderly Park lives history." *The Charlotte Observer,* July 25, 2015. http://www.charlotteobserver.com/news/local/article28702810.html.

Coates, Ta-Nehisi. *We Were Eight Years in Power: An American Tragedy.* New York: One World, 2017.

Durden, Robert F. "Redeemer Democrats." In *Encyclopedia of North Carolina,* edited by William S. Powell. Chapel Hill: University of North Carolina Press, 2006.

Edwards, Brent Hayes. *Epistrophies: Jazz and the Literary Imagination.* Cambridge: Harvard University Press, 2017.

Fullilove, Mindy Thompson. *Root Shock: How Tearing Up City Neighborhoods Hurts America, and What We Can Do About It.* New York: New Village, 2004.

Hanchett, Thomas W. *Sorting Out the New South City: Race, Class, and Urban Development in Charlotte, 1875–1975.* Chapel Hill: University of North Carolina Press, 1998.

Hester, Karlton Edward. "The Melodic and Polyrhythmic Development of John Coltrane's Spontaneous Composition in a Racist Society." *Studies in the History and Interpretation of Music* 54, xxiii–xxiv. Lewiston, NY: Edwin Mellen, 1997.

Holiday, Billie, with William Dufty. *Lady Sings the Blues.* 50th Anniversary Edition. New York: Harlem Moon, 2006.

Hunt, James L. "Fusion of Republicans and Populists." In *Encyclopedia of North Carolina,* edited by William S. Powell. Chapel Hill: University of North Carolina Press, 2006.

Jacobs, Jane. *The Death and Life of Great American Cities.* New York: Vintage, 1992.

Kratt, Mary, and Thomas W. Hanchett. *Legacy: The Myers Park Story.* Third Edition. Charlotte, NC: Myers Park Foundation, 2009.

Noblin, Stuart. "Sydenham Benoni Alexander." *NCpedia.org.* https://www.ncpedia.org/biography/alexander-sydenham-benoni.

Porter, Lewis. *John Coltrane: His Life and Music.* Ann Arbor: University of Michigan Press, 1998.

Reisner, Robert George. *Bird: The Legend of Charlie Parker.* Boston: Da Capo, 1977.

Stephenson, Sam. "Is This Home?" In *Oxford American,* November 10, 2007. http://www.oxfordamerican.org/magazine/item/1331-is-this-home.

Thurman, Howard. *Jesus and the Disinherited.* Boston: Beacon, 1976.

Discography

Coltrane, John. "Alabama." *Coltrane Live at Birdland.* Impulse IMPD-198, 1996, compact disc.

Holiday, Billie. "Strange Fruit." *The Billie Holiday Songbook.* Verve P2-23246, 1986, compact disc.

Monk, Thelonious, and John Coltrane. "Epistrophy." *The Complete 1957 Riverside Recordings.* Riverside Records RCD2-30027-2, 2006, 2 compact discs.

Parker, Charlie. "Just Friends." *Charlie Parker with Strings.* Verve Records MGC–675, 2013, compact disc.

Parker, Charlie. "Thriving from a Riff." *Charlie Parker: The Complete Savoy & Dial Master Takes.* Savoy Jazz SVY 17149, 2002, 3 compact discs.

Preservation Hall Jazz Band. "When the Saints Go Marchin' In." *When the Saints Go Marching In–New Orleans Vol III.* CBS FM38650, 1983, Album.

Rollins, Sonny. "Tenor Madness." *Tenor Madness.* Prestige 7047, 1992, compact disc.

Simone, Nina. "Strange Fruit." *Nina Simone Anthology.* BMG Heritage BH2 53015, 2003. 2 compact discs.

Smith, Bessie. "Backwater Blues." *The Essential Bessie Smith.*Sony Legacy B000002ADO, 1997. 2 Compact Discs.

Made in the USA
Columbia, SC
27 May 2019